I0406871

Live Free

By Jerry Quill

Taking back our nation one dependent at a time

Copyright© Jerry Quill, 2010

Without limiting the rights under copyright reserved above, no part of this publication may be reproduced, stored in or introduced into a retrieval system, or transmitted, in any form, or by any means (electronic, mechanical, photocopying, recording, or otherwise), without the prior written permission of the above copyright owner of this book.

"Thanks to my wonderful wife Janice for her support while writing this book"

Introduction

"The mystery of government is not how Washington works but how to make it stop." **P. J. O'Rourke** (1947)

You are watching your government burn through unimaginable amounts of money. It's pretty clear that your children's and grand children's futures are being squandered right before your eyes. Your political leaders and your media are screaming from the mountain that we haven't even scratched the surface of what needs to be spent to make the planet right…and damn it, you're going to pony up to fix it even if you have to go bankrupt to do it. And you know what? Your leaders are sick and tired of having to plead with you to change the world. You're getting their version of utopia whether you like it or not. You can complain all you want but the movers and shakers in Washington have decided you're too dim-witted to know what's good for you.

You live in a democracy so your vote should count right? But no matter whom you vote for nothing changes. You're always left with a choice between dumb and dumber, and some over paid talking head on TV keeps telling you that questioning the spending habits of your leaders is downright un-American. But you live in the real world and from where you're standing you can see that Washington has gone completely insane. You're to the point where building a fence around The Capitol seems like a whole lot better solution than building one along the Mexican border. Yea, they should fire every last one of those SOBs; a clean sweep come Election Day, and then they'll stop wasting money on all that dumb crap...well except for the fact that the new guys will pick up right where the old guys left off. Meet the new boss; same as the old boss. Don't they get it? Washington just needs to stop spending money.

But wait; your mom is on Medicare and how can she survive without her Social Security? You can't afford to take care of her...not with what you are paying for Medicare, Social Security, local state and federal taxes, sales tax, property tax, and the taxes in the cost of the products you buy. And you can't afford the $5,000 to send your kid to a private school unless you get a tax credit and you can't have that. It would destroy the public education system that's spending $10,000 to only half educate your kid. You can't get rid of government, you need government. You're screwed!

You really believe in the Constitution and you know what Washington is doing is well....Unconstitutional; but Grandma's got to eat and your spouse can't quit the job that pays the family's tax bill so the kids can get home schooled…of course, if that other income could go towards a private school?? But that makes too much sense; the brianiacs in DC won't allow you to. After all it is a free country and somebody's got to be forced into paying for that.

One thing you know for sure is that if they'd let you and the folks from your bowling team run the country you'd have the whole mess cleaned up in a few hours. So you look for a politician who displays just a little of the common sense that your friends and family have, and during the campaign the wannabees from both sides sound pretty sharp. As a matter of fact, they tell you exactly what you wanted to hear. But the minute they get to Washington they flip you off and dive head first into the spending orgy. You feel like Charlie Brown knowing that Lucy is going to pull the ball from under you but next election you line up to kick the ball anyway. You've accepted that reality and now you are willing to vote for whom ever makes the prettiest promises that you know they have no intention of keeping.

The truth is that the government is broken and there is not a damn thing you can do about it right? Wrong, there is something you can do but it will take a long time and you must take some responsibility to fix things. It's called **'Live Free'.**

The concept is simple. Government spending is driving us into financial ruin. Tax hikes on the rich or anybody else won't cover the gap because they reduce economic growth and actually reduce revenue. An extensive reduction in spending is the only logical solution. Spending on education, healthcare and retirement are the biggest parts of our budget. But education, healthcare and retirement can all be purchased privately. The only way to reduce spending is to massively increase the number of Americans that are able to buy their own private plans and drastically reduce government's obligation to provide social assistance to those that can't. Not by making any American to suffer from budget cuts but by making it affordable for people to move to the private sector. They get better quality social programs and the government gets painless spending reduction.

This is not an overnight solution. Most of us over 40 will live our lives and die as government dependents. Change will come from our children. We need to help them Live Free from government dependency. Today 12% of American kids go to private school and 88% are in public schools. Just imagine if those numbers were reversed. Imagine the savings if only 10% went to public schools. Imagine in 65 years if the government provides retirement to only 10% of the population. It will take 20 years for today's newborns to enter adulthood prepared to spend the rest of their lives without needing a penny of government assistance.

We need to see the year 2075. What it could look like. 2 years election cycles suck. It's not enough time to do anything. But 65 years in the future anything is possible. We can build a society where 95% of Americans don't need a government freebie; and that 95% can care for the unfortunate 5% without any government help. Limiting government by leaving them nothing left to do.

And don't expect your government to get on board. They like exactly what they have now. Controlling trillions of dollars means power and after all isn't that the ultimate lure for every politician. Change can't come through legislation; we have to change as a culture. Help our children become independent without the interference or permission of the government.

Living Free is about restructuring our society by refusing to use public schools, by building private alternatives to Medicaid, Medicare and Social Security; not to immediately close those programs but to compete against them and slowly drive them out of business. Living Free is about changing our perception of a just society where every individual can have access to programs that satisfy our basic human needs; not provided by a wasteful and corrupt government bureaucracy but through the free market where the laws of supply and demand give us the highest quality product for the lowest possible price. A society where the government is there to catch those who fall through the cracks but only a miniscule percentage of the population and a pool of needy that society is constantly striving to push into the private sector. Living Free means offering Americans the programs they desire not based on political favoritism but by the value of the service provided to each individual and where free market competition forces providers to constantly increase quality while lowering the costs to retain their customers.

Our government tries to monopolize the dispensing of social programs by driving private providers out of business through unfair business practices that in the private sector would be considered illegal. Their goal is to force as many Americans as possible to become dependent on what only the government can provide no matter how crappy the service or how expensive it is. It has nothing to do with bettering society; it's only about giving power to those in charge of the government. Our government leaders then dole out favors to their supporters and punishment to those that oppose them.

Many of us will not be able to escape our government enslavement and this book is not meant to ask anyone to suffer to live free, but we can begin to create the institutions and cultural mores and traditions that allow our children to escape the clutches of the federal government. It's not about cutting programs and kicking the poor to the streets, it's about building superior private alternatives that compete against government programs and encourage and entice dependents to voluntarily abandon their government stipend. Most importantly, it's about creating the institutions and movement the next generation will use to live a life completely free from dependency. It's about attacking poverty aggressively right at its source…privately. Helping America's poor children into private schools and preparing them for productive prosperous lives to break the cycle of poverty.

Our culture is flawed in two ways. Number one, over our lifetimes our government takes nearly 50% of our earnings in some form of taxation. If our government was using this money to constructively end poverty once and for all the investment could be justified because at some point the end of poverty would mean that this level of taxation would cease and society would be transformed. But our government designs programs that use our hard earned income to perpetuate poverty and actively recruit new citizens into a life of government dependency.

The second problem is that to live independently we need to begin creating and saving wealth from the day we are born and passing back wealth from one generation to the next. Of course, most infants aren't generating an income so they must rely on parents, extended family and the community as a whole to begin the process of saving and educating for a future of independence.

Later in the following chapters I wish to lay out the elements of the 'Live Free' movement and how the movement can begin to grow without the help or interference of the government. But before we begin we should explore the reasons that government has become so intrusive and we should also reflect on the true nature of freedom.

Today we are hopelessly lost in an endless failed attempt to elect politicians that will reform our nation, but it seems impossible to get to a point where common sense reforms will even be considered. The problem is that we seek to elect a politician who will save us from the politician. The reality is that the welfare state is working great…for the politician. Government spending has never been intended to help the poor or even average Americans, it's designed to give power and money to socialist politicians and that part is working just fine. It's simple; give tons of free money to people and hire a lot more people to pass the money out. Get all those people to vote for the politician that promises to keep the whole scheme running.

The politician splits us into groups and leads us into battle against each other. Right and left, rich and poor, black and white, we're all expected to hate each other to the point where stealing each other's money is the only way to address our grievances. But we all have one thing in common: We are being exploited and abused by politicians. So what do we do?

The solution seems pretty simple right? Just elect a bunch of new politicians to Congress and they'll write laws that give the country back to the people. The problem with turning to Congress to attempt reform is that a reform politician will propose a transformation of a social program to be written into law. That reform will require an existing program and its dependents (*point A*) to convert to an unproven, alleged better program (*point B*). To maintain their present level of funding, the administrators of the *Point A* program will vilify the *Point B* legislation and scare all the dependent financial recipients of the present program. The administrative bureaucracy and the social dependents will unite as a voting block and defeat the legislation and no progress will be made.

The reform legislators who proposed the restructuring will then be seen by their supporters as a failure and by the dependency coalition as a threat. In the next election nay votes increase while yea votes wane. Reform politicians lose. This evolutionary process eventually leads to house and senate seats being held by either pro welfare-state Democrats or Republican and Blue Dog Democrats who will 'tolerate' socialist legislation for fear of liberal wrath. The problem with this process of reform is that it requires conservative legislation enacted by the enemy. It's much easier to legislate control then it is to legislate freedom. The Constitution was based on the premise that our freedoms come first, independent of government which steps in later at our invitation to assist us.

The principle that our freedom exists independent of and in spite of government has two distinct aspects to it. The first and most recognizable is that government is not allowed to oppress us and we have a responsibility to act as watchdogs over our government and to get involved to protect the limits that we impose on government to guard our freedom.

The second less considered aspect is our responsibility to construct a society that can freely, without government interference, offer to every single citizen a fair opportunity for a reasonable standard of living. I think we should take this concept one step further: The welfare state has engrained in America the belief that every individual no matter how down trodden is entitled to basic necessities like food, shelter, education, and medical care. Those purists in favor of rugged individualism would see the law of the jungle and survival of the fittest as the true test of ultimate freedom. But human nature makes us wince at the sight of human suffering and we are compelled to try and do something. In the absence of private institutions we satisfy our guilt by dropping our feelings of responsibility at the Capitol steps and sure, they'll pacify us…for a hefty price. America is going to have a welfare system; the idea is not to let the federal government anywhere near it. Therefore a private welfare system is the only answer.

Freedom carries with it a responsibility to create a culture that addresses our collective social demands, and in the absence of legislation, a free society has to develop institutions, mores, traditions and standards of decency that promote self reliance and community involvement. If we accept the concept that society will provide a minimal standard of living for every individual then a free society would have to build private institutions to provide for the needy it accepts responsibility for. If we build superior institutions that encourage poor people give up their low quality government program at the same time offering them the opportunity to advance out of poverty we improve the overall worth of our society while diminishing the power of the government.

If the free market is tasked with providing welfare, it has to be paid for by free citizens. This would require two important cultural demands: To give back to society and be smart philanthropic consumers. Giving benefits to a huge pool of needy underprivileged people is expensive. Government wants to grow that pool because they have a symbiotic relationship where the government provides a sustenance existence in return for a vote. The average self reliant person who ultimately finances that pool wants to shrink it. The goal of the Live Free Movement should be to eliminate poverty. Paying for anti-poverty programs can be very inexpensive when there are no poor people.

Therein lays the superiority of private over government welfare. The government sees poverty as a cash cow. The politician exploits poverty to gain his own personal power and has a strong motive to perpetuate it. The free, wealth creating people that actually pay the costs of welfare have a strong motivation to end poverty. If poverty were eliminated, we'd put that cash back into our pockets. The problem is that a free society also has the option of ignoring poverty, but past experience proves to us that ignoring the problem leads to a bigger problem; government welfare. Since America's productive class pays for the cost of welfare either way, the logical conclusion is that the free market should be incentivized to end poverty as opposed to expecting the government to do so especially when their motivation is to perpetuate and expand poverty.

Self reliance is the cure to government dependency and poverty. As a free society we want to expand self reliance and as philanthropic consumers we should give our money to charities that most efficiently and effectively move individuals from dependency to self reliance. In a vain attempt to elect Republicans, conservatives pump billions of dollars into a political system that wants to undermine self reliance. To try to legislate conservative principles which are supposed to exist beyond government is wrong. That money should be spent striking at the heart of societal problems. Erasing the root causes of poverty and demanding that as many poor people as possible use the avenues society provides to become independent should be our goal. The government won't be able to justify increased spending on a shrinking pool of needy. The money we send today to elect a RINO who can't change a thing in Washington would be much better spent sending poor kids to private schools so they won't be collecting welfare in 25 years.

The answer is not to subsidize poverty to the point where it is in reality 'encouraged', but to develop ways to end it once and for all. One of the most fundamental changes we need to see in a new Live Free society is the expectation that the poor must take

15

responsibility to use the opportunities that society provides for them to advance out of poverty. If poor children are given a free education, society must demand that they take advantage of that education. The dropout rate we see today amongst under privileged children is unacceptable. We blame society but we give a pass to the kids themselves. We think we are being compassionate but in reality we are stealing from these children the lessons in self reliance they more than anyone need to prosper. Education, more than any other thing destroys poverty. Society must demand that every American child reaches adulthood educated and employable. Government education is failing miserably when compared to private education or home schooling. Kicking government out of the education business is a poverty busting idea. Today's politically correct "victimology" is a creation of the leftist ideology that tries to convince the poor that they have no responsibility in their plight. On the surface it's sold as "compassion" but the hard truth is that it's meant to exploit the poor by locking them into dependency while denying them their most effective means of escape; personal responsibility. The left hates the term "personal responsibility" and it's because socialism is dependent on poor people. Without them socialism can't exist. The left understands that personal responsibility destroys poverty and with it the necessity for big government.

Living free is much more than having the government leave you alone, it means stepping up to the plate and taking personal responsibility for yourself, your family and your neighbors and expecting them to do the same. Today the welfare state promotes the idea that all government dependents are "victims" of an unjust society implying that they have no control over their circumstances. They do this to deny a very strong motivation for people to move away from government dependency; shame. To the government, a shrinking pool of welfare collectors is a threat to their power base. If society begins to reject this victim mentality it actually empowers the needy. And if avenues to upward mobility are provided independent of the government, the pool of underprivileged will shrink along with the obligation of caring for them. The notion that an individual is "entitled" to free money from the government has to be replaced by the reality that a government dependent is accepting charity and has an obligation to move as quickly as possible away from being a charity collector to becoming a provider of charity. Pride and shame are very important to a free society.

Government uses the threat of violence with a badge to enforce civilized behavior. A free society needs a strong moral code with a reverence for individual rights to drastically reduce the need for government's ultimate enforcement. Since we as individuals don't have the threat of violence like the state does to enforce our needed social mores, pride and shame become vital tools. And before the promoters of the welfare state call you intolerant for ramming your values down their throats, remember these are the same people who have no problem shaming you about your views on abortion, religion, lower taxes, smoking, immigration, etc.

The politicians in Washington are encouraging then exploiting the poor, using our guilt to get at our money and our freedom. But we don't need permission from the government to live free. We don't need Washington to write thousands of pages of legislation to live free. We are free in spite them. We just have to start living that way and helping others to do the same. Take away their poor people and the government loses power.

I hope to examine in this book a way for average Americans to join together to build a society that begins to eliminate, without the government, the problems that the welfare state exploits to expand their power. We don't have to march on Washington to demand they return our freedom; they can't take our freedom without our consent. We voluntarily surrender our freedom when we accept a government handout. We regain our freedom when we simply say, "Thanks but no thanks"

Chapter 1

Live Free

"Freedom is the greatest fruit of self-sufficiency"
Epicurus (300BC)

'What is it?'

'**Live Free**' is an ideal, a concept. It's an organization and think tank. It's a movement.

The ideal:
That over a long period of time, say 65 years (the retirement age of today's newborns) we end the welfare state by eliminating poverty and voluntarily refusing to use government programs. We can't shrink government if we keep demanding they provide

for us cradle to grave. While the elderly today may not be able to survive without Social Security, today's newborns can. Even if *we* can't get off the dole, we can blaze the path our grand children will use to live free; and not by legislation but through cultural change.

The concept:

The basic idea is for Americans to find ways to provide all their social needs without using any government money. To form social groups to help each other survive and thrive without government assistance. To build markets and protect private companies that cater to our private social needs. To donate to causes that help the needy free themselves from government dependency. To build cultural and societal systems that allow today's newborns to live their entire lives independent of government subsidy and at a higher standard of living.

The organization:

Live Free^{TM} is a non-governmental organization that would work to give direction to those who want to live free. **(Live Free**^{TM} is not an actually trade mark, I'm just showing it this way for effect to distinguish between a movement and an organization). It would provide ideas for trading in your government benefit for a private one, for ways to stay away from government dependency traps and to help free the next generation of children from government dependency. It doesn't tell us what to do; it points us to the different options that we can choose from and puts us in touch with groups and companies that can help us become independent.

The think tank:

Live Free™ does research and compiles information to educate us and develop new innovative ways for us to satisfy our social needs inexpensively. It works as a watchdog against government and industry looking for problems or bad policy that hamper our ability to live free. It develops rating systems to measure how new legislation helps or hurts us to live free. It uses the power of the Live Free community to pressure Congress and state governments to enact 'Live Free' friendly legislation. It gives a 'Live Free' rating to private companies so we as consumers can apply pressure to businesses to extract themselves from Washington politics and subsidies. Diverting money away from the Washington sink hole and towards a frontal attack on poverty…funded privately.

The Movement:

The movement is Americans banding together in a common cause and a common direction to change our country, our government and our culture; to advance the nation's and our own personal freedom and prosperity. Not to win the next election but to transform humanity in the next half century. Whether you belong to a group that promotes the Live Free concept or if you just do your part on your own, if you believe in self reliance and rolling back government dependency you are part of the movement.

'Where do we start?'

We start by building a dream… a goal, a vision. We need to pick a date, 2075; the retirement age of today's newborns. We can imagine an ideal country or world for that matter; to dream of real change…not politically but culturally. Of course everybody's "Vision 2075" will be different, but if we can agree on some very basic principles our combined vision will allow us to work in concert to reach our destination.

A society based on free individuals creating a poverty free culture with the most limited government involvement possible can't rely on legislation to succeed. It needs the culture to change from within. It needs clearly defined direction and goals and it needs demanded and respected moral standards for individuals to live by; both by those providing opportunities out of poverty and those poor expected to use those opportunities. Changing the nation's victimology culture will not be easy; therefore it will take aggressive long-term dedication from the movement's members and leaders. It will also take combined and efficient grass root organization.

I'm proposing an organization I call **Live Free**™ devoted to privatizing the welfare state. This organization would be an umbrella group for all the non-government entities working to shrink the government. It would help suggest overall long term goals towards national independence and help these entities work more efficiently together. Of course the movement transcends any one group. It needs to be a mindset; a way of life. And considering it would be made of millions of free individuals, each contributing in their own unique way, who knows how it would evolve. But by keeping an eye on the dream great things can be accomplished.

Live Free™ would articulate the basic principles of freedom in relation to the obligation of providing "social justice" through the free market and by reminding all free people that ignoring the needy leaves them vulnerable to exploitation by governmental power seekers. **Live Free**™ would begin and promote initiatives that lead the nation towards independence.

I think the most important and relatively easy way to start would be an initiative to encourage Americans to open IRAs for every newborn. We could call them "IRAs for Life". Ironically Hillary Clinton stumbled on this concept during the 2008 primary race against Barak Obama. She proposed a $1,000 government funded IRA account for every newborn. She was attracted by the government funding part but someone took her aside and explained to her that the IRA part would destroy the welfare state. Within 48 hours she quickly and quietly rescinded her proposal.

This would be a great first task for the newly anointed **Live Free**[TM] Organization

IRA for Life:

Retirement is something children are unaware of, 20 and 30 year olds don't think about much, 40 and 50 year olds worry about and something retirees are too often unprepared for. But what all retirees know is that if they had started saving from the day they were born they'd be a lot better off. Social Security exists to fix the mistake of not saving early enough. It's easy to see that fixing Social Security is a fundamentally flawed proposition. When S.S. was started 10 workers were paying for 1 retiree, in the future with the aging of the Baby Boomers it will become a one to one ratio between workers and retirees. That's unsustainable. It's just simple demographics. What's needed is an essential cultural change that encourages retirement savings earlier in life by creating programs that take advantage of the wealth building opportunity of the 65 years before retirement.

The retirement payout by Social Security can in no way match the earning potential that well managed private retirements can offer. The main selling point of S.S is the security part. It's knowing that your income will be there way into the future because it's backed by the government, but even that reassurance is waning today. Looking at the market down turn of 2008 it's understandable that many would be weary of private retirement, but private retirement can be fortified. With proper private insurance, sane regulation and adequate capitalization, economic down turns and unforeseen events can be anticipated and prepared for. What's needed is a concept that promotes starting your retirement savings from the day you are born and encouraging the anticipation of retiring without governmental contributions.

It works like this: IRAs for children are offered with an initial investment of $10, $20 or $50. At birth, new parents open an IRA account for their newborn's retirement (with no government contribution and without a government mandate). Then we begin a new American tradition – Donating to a child's IRA as a gift –

Relatives come to visit a new mother they bring an IRA donation as a gift. Birthdays, holidays, graduations, an IRA gift. Mowing the lawn, chores, part goes in the IRA. Volunteerism for teenagers, military service, the Peace Corps, all contribute to the IRA. Around 10 or 11 years old it becomes traditional that kids get a small portion of their IRA and dabble a little in the stock market, helping them to become better educated about basic economics, how wealth is created, and how their IRA works. Most children and way too many adults are ignorant of the most basic economic principles. This makes them highly susceptible to the false sales pitch from the big government proponents searching for dependents. As the culture begins to accept the importance of children's IRAs, society will find new and creative ways to fund those IRAs.

Young people would be given an opportunity to earn IRA contributions for all kinds of civic service volunteerism or scholastic rewards for good grades. And look, we hear over and over that Americans don't save enough, this is a perfect solution. Kids grow up with the experience that saving is a natural part of life. This is a cultural change. From the earliest age a new generation becomes aware and participates in the welfare of their own future. They learn the foundation of good financial planning and the principles of personal responsibility. Too many

Americans today take pride that they can "play the system". The real pride should be taken in 'avoiding' the system.

As we become young adults, we were raised managing our IRAs so that in our 20s we enter the work force as better educated and financially suave investors bargaining with our employers for juicy IRA plans as part of our overall compensation. The money companies spend for taxes or union benefit packages can be diverted into employee IRAs. When someone leaves a company they take their IRA with them. The business gets to make a clean break and not be saddled with retirement legacy costs. The employees don't lose their pension fund if the company goes belly up. As the importance of private IRAs grows, employers will take the opportunity of enhancing employee IRAs as a compensation bargaining chip, like matching direct deposits into the separate IRAs of each family member including children.

It's this second generation where 'IRAs for Life' begins to take off. Hopefully this is where welfare state and class warfare propaganda begin to subside. Obsolete 100 year old government programs will be held up against modern efficient private social programs and exposed as harmful. The pool of government dependents that socialist politicians rely on to get elected will be drastically shrinking while the voting block of people who demand governmental spending be diverted into their private accounts will be exploding. The demographic shift from government dependents to non-dependents will be clear and the politician who wants to stay in power will have no choice but to respond.

We can use our IRAs to finance our college educations or to buy homes, both being great investments that eventually impact our retirement. It can be used to leverage private medical insurance policies. You could put $5,000 in a liquid money market to use as a potential deductible, reducing the premium on a medical policy. Employers and employees work together to build wealth for both. Employees can personalize their compensation packages to maximize their unique investment goals.

If you start an IRA at birth and contribute $25 per month with a modest 6% average growth rate, when the child reaches 20 years old they'll have $11,500 as a beginning nest egg. $35 at 8% generates $20,600.

Using your IRA to finance your education is a good investment, hopefully increasing what you can contribute the rest of your life. But if you keep your $11,000 in your IRA and contribute $150 per month at 6% for 45 years you'll retire at 65 with over $580,000. But it's important to remember that you're helping to eliminate the Social Security system, reducing government spending and your tax obligation. By the time you add up federal, state and local income taxes, sales tax, gas taxes, property taxes and pay the higher prices for the tax on the products you buy, Americans can pay 40-50% in taxes.

If you make $36,000 a year you could be paying more than $14,000 in taxes per year. (Hiding the taxes you pay is an art form to the socialist politician.) If you could reduce that tax burden by 20% you'd put $2800 per year or $240 per month in your pocket. If you invested your $240 in your IRA you'd retire with $830,000 in your account. These small contribution numbers begin to generate the retirement income that takes you over the threshold of reformed S.S. eligibility.

As people become more dependent on the private IRA and away from S.S. dependency, the campaigns of politicians will change also. The day will come when politicians will be running on a ticket of enhancing your private IRA instead of pitching direct government handouts. No longer will they generate fear by saying "The other guy wants to take away your Social Security!" The fear mongering will be "The other guy wants to raid your IRA" That campaign will be good for America.

One stipulation should be that each and every IRA pays an insurance premium which covers an overall safety net cost that protects against individual IRAs that fail to meet the government's minimum income requirements. Basically the Social Security system is first means tested and then gradually converted to private insurance backed by something similar to the FDIC type insurance. Economic down turns do pose a problem with private retirement funds but they also pose problems for S.S., it's just that the Treasury can borrow money to ride the storm out. But comprehensive protections can be built into the system. Proper private insurance along with a government failsafe and sane-regulation that keeps everything capitalized properly can overcome economic slumps.

The problem with government programs today is that they micro manage every last dollar that goes to their dependents. That's a tremendously costly administrative feat.....and wasteful. Because this bureaucracy is a monopoly they are slow to adopt management technology that put the private sector light years ahead. They are also rampant with corruption and graft. The role of government should be to back a handful of insurance companies and pump in large sums of money if needed; like a FDIC for IRAs. The government would save billions of dollars in administrative costs if it had to only write 10 checks even though those checks might be quite large. It would save trillions of dollars if they only had to write those checks once every 70 years. Ideally it should never come to this though. If insurance is designed to anticipate normal economic down turns and if government can enact sane-regulation that heads off dangerous economic trends like bubbles in certain industries, real security could be reached. If the government unshackles itself from the micromanagement of the entire nanny-state apparatus it has erected, it would have the ability to be effective at the job it was originally designed to do; protect individual freedom, enforce the law and protect the homeland. And if the US government wasn't financially strapped by the debt of running the welfare state it would occasionally be able to step in during a crisis to shore up the economy efficiently without threatening to go bankrupt or nationalizing huge sectors of the economy.

The IRA becomes the heart of people's shift to self reliance. Whether rich or poor, every American at least has the vehicle for wealth creation. Even if the government initially wanted to subsidize the IRAs of the poor it wouldn't be a bad thing. Since an IRA, no matter how it is funded, leads to independence. Those government subsidies would lead to their own demise. The government can't fund the poor if there are no poor left. The program dies from obsolescence. Direct subsidies to the IRAs of the poor would be a transitional policy, destine to die when poverty is eliminated. Today's welfare programs are perpetual and never ending.

We hear the horror stories of workers with pensions that disappear when a company goes bankrupt. The difference is that you own your IRA: It's yours. Workers will negotiate transfers of company pensions to 401Ks or IRAs. If a company goes belly up you still own your retirement account. And you can pass down the wealth you've created to your heirs. Future generations of newborns will open their new IRAs for Life with healthy inheritances from Grandma and Grandpa. Today the welfare state encourages generational dependency and poverty. By eliminating the Inheritance Tax and providing incentives for passing down wealth, IRAs strengthen from generation to generation, shifting much of the burden of societal welfare from the government to the family.

So, with a focus on individual wealth creation to eliminate poverty (which allows more personal investment in the future), and proper insurance and capitalization of the system and the economy, and with generational wealth enhancement, a private retirement culture can reach a realistic point of security. And it's a given that a small number of citizens will be unable to care for themselves in the private arena. At that point the government can step in and be the protector of last resort. But even then, with the socialist establishment dismantled, it would be wiser for the government to administer the programs privately while they only fund it. And considering the huge rise in per capita wealth amongst the population and the reduced taxation demands of the long gone welfare state, charitable contributions could mesh with the government in providing a higher standard of living for the truly needy.

'IRAs for Life' doesn't need some impossible to pass legislation with a huge campaign by leftists to try to demonize and slander anyone associated with this threat to their welfare state. IRAs for children exist today. Many parents already have them for their kids. The point is to expand it and push for every American child to have one.

'Begin the Journey'

It begins with a group of prominent citizens who approach stock brokerages and convince them to offer no or low deposit IRA accounts for all newborns or all minors for that matter. It's great for the brokerages because they are getting new customers they wouldn't likely see for another 30 or 40 years. Any initial cost to brokers for starting so many small accounts will be overcome within the first year or two while the accounts are being funded, and then the brokerages could gleefully look forward to 64 years of new profitable clients. These new accounts will create a market for new mutual funds that cater to these new customers, designed for their needs of retirement 65 years in the future: EXTRA-long-term growth mutual funds. A very valid case can be made that initially unfunded IRA accounts would be extremely profitable for brokerages in the long run. Brokerages would make offers for new parents to come on down and they'll do all the paper work for filing your kid's Social Security forms. I can see the point where brokerages offer $50 for opening new accounts the way banks do for new savings accounts.

I envision people like Newt Gingrich, Bill Bennett, and many other leading conservative folk sitting down with the CEOs of Scottrade, E-Trade and others and designing IRA accounts that can be opened for free for children. The parents of children will go to their local brokerage office and the brokers will help them file their S.S. forms and open their accounts. This is just the first step to setup the ground work for this project. It's important to understand that these small actions are the seeds that will eventually change the American culture decades into the future. And this is the fundamental goal of the Live Free Movement; changing the culture.

Live Free™ would start an advertising campaign to urge Grandma and Aunt Sally to put $25 or $50 in the account as gifts for the kids throughout the year. Make small contributions and hopefully after the first year the vast majority of accounts will surpass the $500 limits the brokerages impose today to open an account. After 3 or 4 years do the "Year of the Total Enrollment Campaign" A year of barraging the media about enrolling every child in an IRA and educating the public on the new tradition of IRA gifts and about the importance of small but consistent monthly contributions. If it gets to the point where getting your kids immunized and setting up their IRA is on the same level of importance then the battle is won. No Child Left Behind (without an IRA) should be the battle cry of this movement. Again, none of this is done with the need for legislation. Cut the politician out of the loop.

The "**Original Birthday Gift**" would play a huge part. All brokerages would provide IRA "gift certificates" that would be interchangeable at any brokerage. They would only be good for opening a newborn's IRA. Make it a tradition that upon the birth of a new child family, friends, neighbors, co-workers, church members…anyone closely related gives a small IRA gift certificate. New parents would be sitting on a stack of hundreds of dollars worth of certificates that can *only* be redeemed by opening an IRA for their newborn. This tradition would drastically and quickly change the culture.

It's also important to consider that investing into an IRA puts capital into the economy.

4,315,000 children (or potential brokerage firm customers) were born in the US in 2007. If each child per capita were receiving $25 per month in their IRA after a year they'd have added just under $103 billion of capital to the world economy. Over 10 years, assuming 4.3 million births every year and a $25 per capita monthly contribution by kids under 10, the capital investment in the global economy reaches a staggering $7.1 trillion, after 20 years its $27.1 trillion. Capital investment creates jobs which steal government dependents from the socialists. Children would actually affect the job market they will be entering into; they will be creating their own jobs. As job increases out strip available employees, employers have to offer better compensation....like bigger contributions to your IRA.

And as the world economy grows poverty shrinks. Poverty has a cost to developed countries which eventually gets spread out amongst its citizens, and as global poverty decreases the individual cost burden per capita to our children and our selves shrink. As the formerly poor become middle class they demand more products and services which create jobs that grow our IRAs.

It's important to remember that an "IRA for Life" account is a 65 year venture; you must be able to imagine what that future will look like. If we consider the trends of the global economy during the last few decades, we watched as industry chased cheap labor around the world. Manufacturing moved to China in search of cheap labor. Now jobs are leaving China headed towards Africa in search of cheap labor there. But the process leaves behind a growing and vibrant middle class....all in need of products and services. At some point in the next half century human cheap labor will begin to run out. At that point the world will begin to use robotic cheap labor and America will be a leader.

A global human labor shortage will lead to higher standards of living and reduced poverty. Reduced poverty will lead to less financial cost for public welfare and leave the population with more to invest in their personal social needs. IRA for Life Accounts, being a major source of capital, will play an important role in the planet's economic evolution, and being non-governmental the model could spread to free markets around the world.

When a person retires financially self reliant they require no transfers of wealth from younger working people allowing the younger generation to have more to invest or to apply to personal social needs, including their IRAs, healthcare and education; not to mention food and shelter. As time passes the private retirement system strengthens. As private retirement becomes more and more important to the average citizen so will the cultural demands for everyone to take advantage of the system. In other words, society will expect individuals to be self reliant and for government to protect the economy that private social programs depend on. Politicians will be elected on their ability to protect the private economy not on doling out pork.

But we need to develop societal standards and mores to accompany our new private culture. Part of changing the culture away from government dependency has to do with outlining what Americans are expected to do as a member of society. It needs to get to the point that parents no matter how rich or poor feel ashamed if they don't have an IRA for their kids, it's just something you do. Today's political correctness culture (the propaganda arm of the socialist ruling class) tries to convince the nation that there should be no shame in being part of 3 or 4 generations of welfare recipients. It's not enough to provide those in poverty with the opportunities for advancement, but as a society we should expect that the poor take personal responsibility to maximize those opportunities and play an active role in the elimination of their own economic short comings. This cultural change in attitude cannot stem from the government especially when its bureaucracy's interests are counter to our objective. Private social advancement will depend on a concerted long term media campaign. All the advertising for privatization should promote the larger ideal of personal responsibility. Just as important is that the individual members of the 'Live Free Movement' understand and can convey the concept of personal responsibility and actively engage the leftist forces who would try to demonize that concept to protect the welfare state. The funding for the advertising could come by diverting money away from donations to political campaigns. Change will come faster by attacking poverty then by electing conservative politicians who end up tolerating government expansion. Many aspiring conservative office seekers who might get elected to only be corrupted or defeated later should be encouraged to join the Live Free Movement outside the government to build private institutions and help dismantle the welfare state.

Personal responsibility can be transformed into a consumer demand. Consumers will feel compelled to purchase those things that society deems necessary to be considered personally responsible. If society deems that providing for your own retirement is an important part of being a good citizen more people will feel obliged to funnel their income into that endeavor. That demand will create a growing market that looks to providing products for these new consumers. The businesses that service those demands will want to expand and they will advertise the principles of personal responsibility that created the market in the first place, which will reinforce those principles and push towards a fundamental change in society's mores. If preparing for retirement from birth becomes expected by society, than the vast majority of parents will conform to those expectations expanding the market for the products that allow them to do so. And because new parents have so many financial restraints with newborns, products will evolve to allow them to enter the market at an initial low cost with the expectation of greater purchases in the future.

In a later chapter I will look more specifically at ways that conservatives can better engage the culture wars and help ingrain conservative principles in to the American fabric with or without the help or hindrance of the governmental elite.

'Why 65 Years?'

The 'Live Free Movement' is not about having to suffer to live free. Most people older than 30 will never be able to live completely free, the Baby Boomer generation is totally lost. And that's OK. But we can do little things that help change the tide, to plant the seeds for long term change. And most importantly we can reach back at help our children and grand children live free. The environmental movement doesn't ask us to sell our cars and move into huts. They point out that just changing some light bulbs or driving a little slower can begin to lower our energy demands. In the same way we need to just plant the seeds and evolve our society slowly over a long period of time. And considering how we've allowed our present government to shovel unimaginable loads of debt onto our children and grandchildren, the least we could do is offer them a way to clean up the mess we've made.

When George Bush introduced a plan to privatize Social Security it was abjectly denounced even though every politician knows that S.S. is in trouble and will eventually have to be privatized, they just want to wait until after their own retirement, once again proving that their own political careers takes precedence over the good of the nation. The problem is that we turned to a politician to fix this dilemma. Politicians can't fix S.S. because its solvency is irrelevant to them. To the politician S.S. is not a retirement program it is a re-election tool, its collapse in 20 or 30 years is immaterial compared to the next general election. Of course those who are going to depend on S.S. in 20 or 30 years will get screwed but today's politician will be comfortably retired by then…and not on S.S.

'IRAs for Life' doesn't need the permission of a politician to begin. In reality it already exists but is just not used enough.

While the socialist politician will recognize childhood IRAs as a threat for the welfare state in the future, attacking childhood IRAs today means attacking all IRAs and will have political ramifications. A politician will not risk his present political career to save the rear end of some future politician. When re-election is king even socialism is expendable. And that's how we fight back. No big programs or initiatives, just the planting of seeds too small for the present ruling elite to risk their careers on; seeds that grow into future independence but also grow the political base that protects the programs. As private retirement expands so does the voting bloc that wants it protected. And we can plant many of these seeds throughout our society changing our entire social fabric, cultivating a forest of independence, self reliance and privatization.

'Why Live Free?'

We Live Free because to do so is the real definition of social justice. By living free we allow ourselves to be givers not takers. By providing for ourselves we free society to care for someone else. Our independence unburdens society. It's all about creating personal wealth as the road to personal freedom, creating a society and culture where each individual has the means to provide for their own education, their own healthcare and their own retirement without expecting the government to forcibly confiscate the wealth of another individual: Where each individual takes the responsibility to pull their own weight.

Modern liberalism gives a lot of lip service to the concept of altruism, self sacrifice towards the service of others, but where is the altruism in demanding benefits for yourself from the labors of someone else? Where is the self sacrifice in expecting a 35 year old with 3 kids to pay for your retirement? Can you be truly altruistic if you don't first provide for yourself? For every dollar you collect as a government benefit there is another dollar in cost to confiscate that dollar and then deliver it to you. And that is two dollars now unavailable for another individual to put towards their personal independence. Providing for yourself is the first and most important contribution you can make to society and is the primary act of altruism an individual can make. If you choose to live a severely austere life style and then donate your wealth or labor to help the needy than bless you; but only if your chosen life style does not require a government subsidy.

The liberal concept of 'the redistribution of wealth as social justice' is a flawed concept. It assumes a lack of control over the creation of wealth. Every individual has the potential to create wealth and every individual needs to expend wealth in order to survive. The elimination of poverty and social justice can only be achieved through the creation of wealth. Modern socialism hampers the creation of wealth and modern liberal dogma stigmatizes individuals who seek to become wealth creators even though wealth creation is the ultimate act of social justice.

Governmental socialism is a perversion bordering on criminality because it exploits the ideals of social justice for the sole purpose of providing power to an elite ruling class. Politicians use needy people who they've helped trap into poverty to cement the politician's power base without giving those that they've trapped into poverty a clear way out.

Living free is about giving every single individual the ability, the knowledge and the opportunity to create wealth throughout their entire lives. From the earliest age all children need to be taught how to create wealth. They should learn right away that they are expected to become self sufficient adults and be provided with every opportunity and tool needed to realize their independence.

An IRA at birth is a tool; a vehicle to create, manage and accumulate wealth throughout an individual's life time. While children need to be protected, they also need to learn how to work and how to generate wealth at an early age so they can reach adulthood on the fast track to independence. Too many kids today are under educated, reach their mid to late 20s and realize they have to go back to school and be re-educated. Now they are thirty something and just beginning to generate the wealth they should have had at 20… and of course they are demanding a government benefit to make up the difference.

But an IRA is not the only answer. Education is a savings account for the mind. And education has to be based on truth to be worth anything. To put a child through 12 years of school that teaches them to hate capitalism and then throw them into the capitalist free market and expect them to thrive is insane. Teaching children the truth about freedom, capitalism and government dependency is critical. Learning that personal independence is the true root to social justice is one of the most important lessons a child can receive.

We can't restore independence over night. Just as we cannot dispel left wing propaganda or disempower the politician in one election. And we must except that a huge portion of today's adults will go to their graves dependent on government. But we can start an evolutionary change. There are specific steps we can take today that begin to give individuals their independence one at a time until it grows into a cultural shift. We can create the traditions and mores that will allow children born this generation to be known as the "Live Free Generation".

'Consumerism: Political Action in the Free Market'

As free people we have a responsibility to manage our society without the interference of our government. If we fail they will step in and do it for us and you can bet it will be in their best interest not ours. While we need adequate and sane regulation that businesses within the free market adhere to, we can also have a tremendous effect by how and where we spend our money. It's called consumerism. Today's socialist movement tries to smear capitalism with the images of the Robber Barons of 150 years ago. Those days are obsolete just as is the socialism of the 1930s. It's a brave new world. We as consumers wield great power in the market place. A company that offends us can be driven out of business in a matter of weeks. We can tame unfettered capitalism. We can demand that businesses uphold our community standards or perish. Earn our respect and then you can earn our dollars. In the information age consumers can punish a company within hours where it might take the government years to do so in court. Many consumer watchdog groups already exist and there's room for many more.

I envision **Live Free**™ playing an important role as a consumer watch dog that monitors the incestuous relations between government and business. Businesses would earn a **Live Free**

Rating (LFR) which is based on a combination of the money they spend on lobbying and what they receive in corporate welfare. Live Free consumers could choose not to spend their money on companies that are in bed with the government. As the movement grows, companies who want to appeal to Live Free members will strive to distance themselves from government. And they'll promote their new independence in their advertizing which will promote the tenets of the Live Free Movement and draw new members into the fold, and thus lead to cultural change without legislation; the main goal of the Live Free Movement.

As Americans abandon government dependency and embrace the free market the economy will grow as will the number of consumers and their disposable income. This in turn will add more incentive for businesses to join the movement. Like with most of our Live Free initiatives, they are able to start out as small steps but are designed to evolved and expand.

Because the Live Free Movement is based on personal responsibility, being a conscientious consumer is very important. And it's not just about products and services we buy. We also want to be good consumers in the charities we donate to. If we are going to transform society we don't want to just contribute to any cause, we want to make sure that the charity helps people advance into independence. A good consumer also needs to follow up and make sure these organizations are living up to their claims. If charities who are successful in moving people out of poverty receive more donations, other charities will try to emulate their success; again, a cultural change without legislation. It would be great to see commercials on TV where a charity brags about how many people they've helped become independent.

It's also important to remember that we are consumers of government benefits. But unlike the free market, we may refuse to accept their product but we are forced to pay for it regardless. And therein lays the failure of the welfare state. The government doesn't have to constantly refine their product. They don't have to add quality to the product or to achieve productivity gains to lower its cost. They only have to perfect the police techniques they use to collect our payments at the end of a gun. But our actions as consumers of government benefits can play a long term role. As we refuse to collect government benefits by purchasing private ones, we reduce the amount of money paid out for any given program. Over a period of time it will either reduce the US deficit or put pressure on the government to reduce taxes. Either way it will help stimulate the overall economy which in turn will increase the flow of individuals from dependence to independence.

What we are trying to achieve is a situation where an individual can take a small action that doesn't require a huge government program or initiative. Then using the ability of social networking that already exists, those individual actions can be multiplied into millions of united actions that begin to affect our culture before the government can even realize what is going on. Death by a thousand cuts, or in our case, a million cuts. If the politician tries to thwart our efforts we can respond within days or weeks where it will take them years to legislate a counter strike. All the while we can attempt to punish the politician at the polls for attempting to interfere with our Live Free initiatives: Opening a two front war against the welfare state.

Once the Live Free Movement is well under way and the organizational abilities are in place, individual members will come up with many new ideas to erode the government's dependency grip. These ideas will be tested on a small scale and if they work they can spread throughout the movement within days. If they provide benefit they will survive and thrive; if not they will simply fade away. No legislation necessary. It's important to remember that we don't want wholesale change overnight. We don't want tens of millions of government workers thrown into the job market all at once. The free market couldn't absorb them and it would cause chaos. We want to transfer them slowly over a long period of time. Our best plans would gently erode the welfare state while gradually expanding the free economy. All our goals need to be long term and evolutionary. Each success breeds more success and bends and twists with the ever changing cultural environment. The specific initiatives set forward in this book are less important than the overall goals and the sense of unity and community the Live Free Movement represents. The individual initiatives are expected to evolve and change or be superseded by better ideas. And this represents the superiority of private over government programs. Politicians will compromise their legislation to attempt to satisfy a variety of constituencies. More often than not they will disappoint all interested parties. In the end the program will be written into stone and become almost impossible to adjust even if the program becomes obsolete or harmful. Bad or destructive ideas in the Live Free world die a quick death when their usefulness expires. 8-track tape manufacturers don't exist today and it didn't take a word of legislation to make that happen.

We as American consumers reign king. We decide which businesses survive or die and that includes our government. It's time we flex our muscles and remind our political leaders who is boss. We've seen our Congressmen drag auto CEOs, oil CEOs, banking CEOs, and publicly spank them while the whole world watched. I think it's about time we do the same to them.

Chapter 2

Education

"Why is it that millions of children who are pushouts or dropouts amount to business as usual in the public schools, while one family educating a child at home becomes a major threat to universal public education and the survival of democracy?" **Stephen Arons**

Education is the true poverty fighter and the most important avenue to advance from government dependence to self sufficiency. It's also the means with which the population uses to maintain their freedom. The principles and requirements of freedom are complex and demand educated free people to protect them. Irrational emotionalism is the enemy of freedom. A government's attempt to monopolize education has been the cornerstone of oppression throughout history. The US control of public education should be carefully scrutinized. The separation between 'School and State' should become a new pillar of freedom.

'Public vs. Private'

The education system has been a prime target of the global socialists for a century now. Conservatives can plainly see that the American public education system has become a socialist manufacturing enterprise churning out little comrades by the millions. Too often reading and math take a back seat to diversity and sex education....and of course, anti-capitalism. Many public school teachers have conflicting interests between their obligations to provide a well balanced objective education and the socialist aspirations of their labor union.

Teacher unions are a small part of a larger leftist coalition that unite many far flung and diversified fringe causes to bring the power of solidarity to the Democratic Party. While many groups are unrelated, they need to support each other to achieve their individual goals. This prompts teacher union members to introduce radical leftist causes to their students as a means of showing solidarity with their larger political movement. The politicians who finance public education also put students second to the needs of their re-election campaigns. They need the support of the teachers unions and if the desires of the teachers unions are in conflict with the needs of students, the students are set aside.

Public education spends on average around $10,000 per student per year while private schools spend just a fraction of that. "But a public education is free!" No its not. It costs $10,000 per year per student. "But why pay for private schools when you don't have to?" Because private school and home school students consistently outperform public school kids. It's the same reason that people buy new Cadillacs when a used Chevy Geo would get them to work and back; quality and value. The public school system is satisfied with graduating students that will conform to the socialist agenda, either as someone excited about paying higher taxes or better yet as a government dependent whose lack of education means they have to sign up and perpetuate the welfare state. But parents have a different dream for their children; to live as independent prosperous individuals self reliant (and maybe having a little cash left over to help Mom and Dad down the road...or at least move out of the house).

Parents will make great sacrifices for their kids, and rescuing them from a failing public school is a priority if not a reality for a huge number of American parents. Barak Obama enjoyed huge support from teachers unions but in the end he had to humiliate them (as do most Washington politicians) by putting his kids in private schools. Even he puts his kids above politics, and rightly so. But the unions support them anyway because they have a dirty little agreement: "We won't put **our** kids into your substandard public schools but we will try to make sure the rest of America is forced to."

But it's not like private education doesn't have a huge foot print in America already. Over 6 million children attend private schools in America. According to the U.S. Department of Education:

- One in four schools in America is private.
- One in nine children attends a private school.
- Private schools save Americans 48 billion dollars annually.
- 90% of private high school graduates attend college, compared to 66% of public high school graduates.
- Private schools are racially, ethnically, and economically diverse. 23% of private school students are students of

color; 28% are from families with annual incomes under
$50,000.

- Private school students consistently outperform public
  school students on standardized achievement tests.

The Live Free movement needs to work closer with groups like
CAPE (Council for American Private Education), a trade group
that aids private schools by helping them pool their resources,
stay on top of industry technology, advertising and promotion
and matching scholarship money with students. Private schools
would benefit from the opportunity for increased enrollment and
the Live Free movement would benefit by reducing the number
of government dependents.

Private education does exist in America and it is growing at a
rapid rate. According to the School Choice Yearbook 2007;
Student enrollment in school choice programs, which include
school voucher programs and scholarship tax credit programs,
has increased 84% over the last 5 years.

The problem now is that tuition rates combined with the tax
burden of funding the public school system puts private
education out of reach for too many Americans. But direct
private school tax credits can solve much of the 'double taxation'
problem. It gives parents a choice to divert taxes they would pay

towards public schools and use it for private school tuitions. Of course the public school teachers unions realize this would devastate their membership numbers and bitterly oppose tax credits, which is why their purchased politicians in Washington drag their feet on reform. But with the success of private and charter school programs and the out of control burdens of the public school budgets, many Democratic legislators both state and national, are allowing privatization programs to move forward albeit slowly.

50 million kids are enrolled on US public schools today. At $10,000 per child, we spend $500 billion for subpar public education. 6 million kids go to private school at about $7,000 per student or $42 billion. If every American child were going to a higher quality school for 7 grand we'd save $168 billion. But more importantly we'd be striking at the heart of poverty. Within a few short years the dropout rate would plummet while test scores would soar. More and more high school grads will be ready for college, vocational training or to enter the work force. You'll also see a reduction in crime and incarceration. When young people have a job they're too damn busy to be getting in trouble. A 17 year old who can't read and has no job is more likely to shoot someone in a robbery and end up in prison. Whether in prison or on welfare, taxpayers have to foot the bill for a failed public school education. That's $100,000 for ten

years of wasted education followed by $400,000 for 20 years of incarceration.

Since the public school system can spend $10,000 per student, that only proves that America as a whole has the means to spend $7,000 per student for a private education. We need to set up new private charities and promote existing private organizations that help subsidize private school tuitions. We should not be against subsidies; just against government subsidies. Hundreds of millions of dollars are raised and spent in presidential elections but $1 million could provide 1000- $1000 tuitions subsidies for private schools. Corporate donations to private school tuitions are extremely wise for businesses. Having a better educated population increases their productivity and profits. And a long term trend of shrinking the burden of government spending would help American businesses to be more competitive globally.

This is where the grass roots of the Live Free Movement can step in and fight the government. If conservatives advance the availability of private education outside the government to the point where it drives public education (with its socialist indoctrination) out of business, the government can throw all the money it wants at public education and it will sit in the treasury's coffers because there is nowhere to spend it. And the Democratic

Party can still pander to the teachers unions except that there will be no teachers union members left to vote for them. While school choice is a wonderful legislative objective, our efforts in no way should end at the steps of the Capitol Building. Increases in private school enrollment will only increase demand for reform. We should see every individual child who transfers from a public school to a private school as a victory. It's also important to see that this is a decades long process. The one advantage we have is the superior product that private schools offer. Parents don't have the leftist desires that teachers unions promote. Parents want their children to be successful and prosperous. Private schools can offer that in a way public schools can't or won't.

'Employability: The poverty fighter'

When an individual graduates with superior job skills, that individual is less likely to use a government social program in his or her future. If that same student has a superior education in the fundamentals of economics, history, and civics he or she will make better choices on Election Day. A highly educated person independent of government freebies is more likely to be politically active in seeking a reduction in their tax burden while expecting common sense productive solutions to social issues....a conservative's dream.

Education, crime and poverty are intrinsically linked. The illiterate and near illiterate are more likely to end up being in poverty or in jail...or worse yet, bound for jail but still on the streets. At the same time the public education systems in the poorest communities continue to increase their spending (mostly on administration...not so much for the students) while a huge percentage of the community's most valued treasures leave school under educated, unemployable and destined for poverty. The public school advocates deny responsibility blaming society or parents for this failure, yet they conveniently ignore the fact that private schools are able to get the job done (and for less money) in the same environment. The public school system like any government bureaucracy is a high paying jobs program for administrators and teachers. The education of children is down further on the priority list. When you watch failed school systems head for bankruptcy like in Detroit or DC, the first thing to suffer is the quality of education followed by maintenance and service staff. Teachers and administrators hang on to their piece of the pie to the bitter end.

Every student that enters the private school system is one less student the government funds. But don't count on government to match their falling enrollment numbers with corresponding budget cuts. Washington will initially see it as an opportunity to raise individual per student expenditures, but as history has shown, throwing more money at education doesn't improve test scores. The inclination of the socialist to just increase spending instead of fixing structural flaws to the system will eventually lead to their downfall. The problem with public education is that the quality of their product is secondary to advancing their political agenda and they are unconcerned with satisfying the demands of their customers; parents. Parents will seek the higher quality product. We must squelch the government's monopoly on the market.

Again, while we have to consider the relationship between government and education, it's only because of their entrenchment in America's educational system. Our relationship to government should be focused on pushing them away. One of the arguments of socialist educational system is access for the poor. The left claims that those who don't have the tuition to attend a private school need a public school system. This is where conservatives bring up the voucher argument. A voucher system is where parents are allowed to pick a school and the funds that would otherwise go to the local public school follow the student.

In reality vouchers already exist. Tax payer funds are allocated to students; it's just that parents have no say in where the money is spent. It goes to the public school where the student lives without regard to the performance of that school. School choice vouchers controlled by the parent not the politician allow private schools to compete for those funds. Purists will argue that the federal government has no business in education in any form including school choice vouchers but we must consider where we are at. A journey no matter how long must start with a first step. Government funded but parent controlled vouchers will break the strangle hold of the teachers unions and open the door for non-government ideas like tax credits to expand. Moving from public to private funding for education is a journey. Setting up the markets to allow this transfer to evolve naturally and gradually is paramount. Parents with vouchers no matter where they get them become consumers with disposable income. This is where the market is grown. Private enterprise will fill the vacuum to help those parents spend that money. If public schools want any of that cash they will have to both increase their quality and lower their prices otherwise their members will have to go seek work at the new private schools springing up.

————————————

'Using what we have'

There are private vouchers; of course the idea is not new. They call them scholarships. Ideally we want third party and corporate tax credits so the wealthy can provide scholarships for the poor. There are organizations that arrange available private school scholarships with needy students like NAIS (National Association of Independent Schools). Third party direct tax credits would greatly expand their market. If we start targeting the nation's poorest and most at risk children to a private education, we are making a frontal assault on poverty. American corporations spend hundreds of millions of dollars supporting political campaigns or paying extortion money to political agitators like ACORN, Jesse Jackson or Al Sharpton. They claim to represent some fake social justice but imagine if that money were diverted to allowing poor kids to become truly employable and independent. Imagine corporations investing in real change not the faux politically correct change peddled by welfare state leaches.

Another source of private school funding is endowments. Where money is donated as a principle investment and the interest from the principle is assigned to provide tuitions in perpetuity. Endowments could be set up to target specific communities or incomes. Endowments could also be set up to allow continual contributions allowing them to expand. A program that was successful would attract new investors to grow the principle of the endowment. For example: A wealthy benefactor or a Live Free organization might start an endowment to provide private school vouchers to the poorest kids in DC. At first it may only be able to provide 100 vouchers but it can do so forever without future funds. If it is successful it would attract donations to expand the principle and in 20 years it might be able to provide thousands of private vouchers. The day could come 65 years from now where all of America's education funding could come from the interest on investments allowing future generations free education for perpetuity.

Sane regulation would provide protection for the endowment and require amends for the changing or disbursement of the endowment if it becomes obsolete in the future. For example: If our DC endowment found that 40 years from now no more poor kid qualified for tuitions because poverty had been eliminated, the bylaws of the endowment would provide for either new targets or a dismantling of the fund. If an endowment didn't have an obsolescence alternative in its bylaws and was unused for a set period like 5 or 10 years it would go into a general endowment fund and be spread out to other functioning endowments.

The endowment idea could be expanded beyond education into transportation and healthcare, but we'll discuss that in later chapters

---

'How to make it work'

So far we see the privatization of education moving slowly forward on its own. Even with the socialist state trying to monopolize education and throwing up road blocks where it can, it can't stop this forward progress because private schools are so superior that resistance is futile. But the Live Free Movement can accelerate the collapse of socialist education in America if it gets focused and attacks at the welfare state's weakest links. If we were to target public education's most vulnerable school systems we could dramatically show the possibilities of private education while at the same time having the most positive social impact possible. America's worst public school systems are in the most poverty stricken urban areas, (and ironically have the highest per student expenditures with the lowest test scores and the highest dropout rates). These socialist institutions would be the easiest to topple with limited resources while allowing quality education to fight poverty in some of America's most needy communities.

For example: The Detroit Public School System is chronically on the verge of collapse. Their enrollment has been steadily dropping for decades. But in Detroit charter and private school demand is increasing. In 1990 Archbishop Adam Maida made a challenge at the Detroit Economic Club. He inspired the creation of Cornerstone Schools, a private school that today has 657 students. While students are charged tuition, Cornerstone Schools is also sponsored by The Detroit Tigers, DTE Energy and The Yazaki Corporation and has a serious advertising campaign with TV pitches by professional athletes to subsidies tuitions that allow lower income students to attend a private school. This is a model that needs to be enlarged.

If an emphasis can be placed on a public to private transfer in Detroit, at some point the public school system will collapse under its own weight; it's right on the verge today. But this could be a good thing. For a public school system to exist it would have to rise from the ashes and match the productivity and academic standards of its private competitors. The Detroit school system would have to rebuild itself. At this point it might be better for the school system to seek private or community funding and forego federal funding and the costly strings it attaches. With the collapse of the Detroit public school system the state of Michigan would have to step in and take over the system but the state is having its own financial difficulties. It would be left with a choice to restart the public school system at $10,000+ per student or simply offer $7,000 dollar per student school choice vouchers. Socialist ideals meet financial reality. Maybe the citizens of Michigan could step in themselves and through the ballot initiative demand that the money raised for public schools from the state lottery be diverted into parent controlled school vouchers.

As the public school system lies dormant conservatives can help private schools fill the void left behind by developing grass roots organizations that help Detroit's children transfer to private schools; a right wing version of ACORN. If the public school system does make a comeback, hopefully it will be as a small player in the overall education market…and having to compete not monopolize and having to please parents to attract income not distant politicians.

Collapsing the Detroit Public School system and then watching Detroit student's test scores and graduation rates rise would be a huge political selling point for private education. And again it's important to point out that a high school graduate is less likely to turn to future welfare than a drop out. And if the private school movement adopts its own version of "No Child Left Behind" Where every Detroit child becomes educated and employable then the city and the region will be transformed. The cost for police protection would be drastically reduced. Less cost for jails. City services for the needy could be slashed. The city's tax base could expand. Detroit's bottom line would surge into the black. Also, private schools don't have a vested interest in promoting class welfare hatred and anti-capitalism to prop up the socialist bureaucracy thus giving private school graduates a much healthier attitude as a productive participant in the workforce. If conservative benefactors focus their donations to specific schools that best support their conservative values they create a market for schools that promote conservative ideals.

It's all about creating a market. While low income parents might have a desire to give their children superior private education, it doesn't become an actionable economic demand until it can be paid for. A poor parent without tuition cannot affect the market. By privately subsidizing tuitions, it puts the control of money in the hands of poor parents which private schools then can compete for; it creates a market. Private subsidization gives poor parents actionable demand, and then the free market can step in to meet it. In essence you are capitalizing the demand side of the equation, converting the ideal of social advancement into a sellable commodity to be serviced by the private sector. As they move up the economic ladder parents become better able to shoulder a greater share of the cost of private tuition so sometimes even a small contribution to a family can make it possible to transfer from public to private schools.

Private schools are more flexible and can design programs that detect and deal with learning and discipline problems before they escalate to a student dropping out. Unlike public schools who get more money thrown at them when they perform badly, private schools with high dropout rates and low test scores will be shunned by parents. Private schools have an incentive to detect learning and discipline problems early and to develop programs to turn these students around quickly. More importantly they are better able to shield the students who want to learn and create a superior atmosphere for the majority of attentive students. Public school financing is not directly tied to an individual student's success. A parent who is dissatisfied with the performance of a public school can't automatically cut off funding to that school...except to go to a private school. Public schools are saddled with minutia like The Model School Disciplinary Code issued by Harvard University were students with disciplinary problems are afforded "due process" which make discipline troublesome for the teachers and allows problem students to interfere with the educations of all their fellow students. A student in a public school has a 5% chance of being harmed with a deadly weapon. And every minute a student is engaged in politically correct fluff is a minute they aren't learning basic math, science, reading and writing.

The idea is to have less emphasis placed on political correct conformity and more placed on future employability. With a dominate private school system you'll see innovation and increased productivity in teaching. In the long term you'll have a much more educated and prosperous population. If you take the vast majority of lower income children and make them highly employable, it will drastically reduce the number of dependents available for exploitation by the government welfare system, and dramatically reduce poverty levels. As more people pay for welfare and less people collect welfare, the overall cost to each individual decreases. As public school systems begin to crumble under their own weight, demand will increase for higher quality education offered by private schools, applying force to increase the supply of private education.

Not all public school systems are necessarily failing. A few miles from Detroit is the Farmington Public Education System, one of the best in the country; but at what cost? If it costs twice as much to just equal the test scores of a private school then can you say that it's better? But at this point in time with limited resources due to the unavailability of tax credits for tuitions we must pick our battles.

'Slaying the Dragon'

If we are looking at the evolution of privatization over a 65 year span, the conversion from public to private schooling will go through phases. The first phase is to use private vouchers to eat away at public enrollment and hopefully collapse a few of America's worst public school systems. But there also needs to be a concerted effort to promote and market the superior quality of private education. If an emphasis can be placed on failing systems in poor urban areas like Detroit or Washington D.C., there will be a double payoff. First, as those public school systems begin to crumble you will bring direct national attention to the private school cause. Secondly, as students living in poverty become better educated they will lead to less poverty as they become employable adults.

Breaking the backs of just a few of America's worst public school systems will change the whole debate. Proving that a large urban area can first survive and then flourish without public schools will be eye opening. Also the loss of membership and clout of the teachers unions will reduce the influence they have on their purchased politicians.

The promotion and defense of the push to target at risk students for private school enrollment has to be strong and deeply layered. Any attempt at interference by the left has to generate a massive outcry that they are being "mean spirited" and "anti-poor". It has to be pointed out over and over again how hypocritical it is for leftist politicians to deny the private education to poor people that their own children enjoy. If President Obama's kids can go to private school, than so should every American child. Like with all aspects of privatization, marketing is everything. All the code words have to be in place. The talking points have to be passed around. All the members of the coalition have to be onboard and ready for battle. These are the tactics the left has used for nearly a century and it's worked quite well for them. We should learn from their success.

I can see the advertisements during election season now; "Don't give your money to any politician's campaign, instead give it to a charitable scholarship program: Bring real hope and change to America! (I'm Joe America and I'm not running for any political office but I still approve this message)" Or how about a bumper sticker that reads: "Donating to a RINO creates a future WINO/ Donate to a private school education instead."

If you consider that education reduces poverty, which reduces government dependency which reduces Democratic voting rolls, then spending RNC advertizing money on privatization commercials makes sense...maybe not in the next election cycle but in the long run. And let's face it; the Republican Party has lost much of its vision. It has some lofty abstract principles it gives occasional lip service to but then it concocts a 'Democrat-Lite' platform to pander to the next election. It then spends hundreds of millions of dollars only to be out socialized by the real socialists. But if you take that same money and invest it in making fundamental changes in the structure of American society like private education, you can create visible concrete substance to those conservative ideals while at the same time knocking down the house of cards that the socialists have built their movement on, crafting a long term place for conservatism and in American politics.

———————————

'Get the State to fight the Feds'

The second phase in the long term struggle is to wrestle away control of all education from Washington and returned it to the states. The continued erosion of public school enrollment will weaken the socialist education lobby and eventually lead to the dismantling of the Education Department and a lessening of federal spending on education. Nationalized education is wasteful and expensive. When those dollars are transferred to the states the citizens have a better ability to influence education spending. A state that drastically reduces its spending by transferring from public to private education lowers its overall tax burden and increases its competiveness with higher quality education at a lower cost.

If approached from a long term point of view, a state can profit by eliminating the federal ties to its schools. If a state refuses federal money for education and then demands that schools divert their curriculum away from political correctness and anti-capitalism and puts an emphasis on employability and wealth creation, over time it can transform its population into more prosperous individuals while drastically reducing its future obligations to provide services to a large pool of under educated poor while at the same time increasing the pool of prosperous tax payers.

Citizens have options in a state that they don't have against the federal government. One of them is the ballot initiative. Imagine a comprehensive education reform initiative that requires:

1. A rejection of federal education dollars along with the attached strings.
2. A curriculum change away from political correctness and socialist indoctrination and an emphasis on free market capitalist employability.
3. Transfer of Lottery profits away from public education and into private school vouchers.

A state that adopts reforms creates a competitive advantage over other states. As its population becomes more employable they become more prosperous expanding the wealth of the state to pay for the services it provides. At the same time it reduces its poverty based obligations to provide social services and police protection. So the state can offer higher quality services, a lower tax burden and a better educated work force thus attracting new businesses and greater economic growth, which perpetuates the cycle. Other states would have to emulate this model or be left at a competitive disadvantage.

The Live Free movement can help this process by working with grass roots organizations on the state level to encourage these reforms accepting victory one state at a time. Once a state has abandoned its federal government addiction, that individual state will be in a better position to enact pro-private school reforms. As more states abandon Washington it reduces the political power of the national teachers unions. As the voting block of pro-private school voters increase and pro-public school voters decrease, the socialist politician (who values his own political power above all else) will turn its back on socialized education and try to cater to the demands of the private school voting bloc...or better yet they might just abandon nationalized education altogether. The socialists won't support a group that is causing them a net loss in votes.

'Socialist education; philosophically'

One aspect that is often overlooked in the public vs. private education debate is the education itself. Over the last 50 years the socialist public school system has slowly abandoned classical Western education in favor of contemporary diversity education. Yet there is no body of research or evidence that diversity education is superior to classical education. As a matter of fact, there is evidence that classical education is superior. The Department of Education study NCES 2008-016 found that in testing among industrialized nations, US publically educated students consistently scores near the bottom in math and science. So if the socialist education system were objectively dedicated to the welfare of their students wouldn't the abandonment of classical education be extensively studied and debated? The reality is that classical Western education is a threat to the socialist state. Classical education is rooted in providing its students with objective reasoning and critical examination skills. The socialist state is sold through the claim of benefit to the citizen but it is designed to benefit the political leadership. If a majority of Americans had the ability to critically examine socialism its flaws would be understood and it would be abandoned. The survival of socialism depends on the inability of its dependents to examine it.

One of the most important aspects for the advancement of privatization is the spread of classical education. Privatization is based on personal responsibility. Personal responsibility depends on the individual making choices that provide maximum benefit both personally and for society. A classical education gives the tools to make more logical and wiser decisions thus improving the individual's value to the community. An important part of being a good citizen in a privatized community is to be self reliant. Wiser choices through truth based applied logic are important to achieving self reliance.

Since the socialist state can't survive the scrutiny of logical reasoning it must minimize the ability to use logic. But while its goal is to protect its own survival, there are unintended consequences. Someone who was not taught the ability to critically examine the welfare state most likely does not possess the tools for making other good life choices and is less likely to be self reliant.

Private schools are not burdened with the task of under-educating its students to hide its flaws. It can choose classical education based on its merit alone: Its only motivation is to attract parents who want the best education possible for their children. Of course the socialists will fight back. As they lose access to more and more students they will seek to control the curriculum of private schools. This is where the Live Free Movement needs to stand firm. The separation of curriculum and state is paramount. The Live Free Movement would have to unite and battle any and all leftist legislation designed to damage private educational freedom. While the market place can protect private education from the damaging effects of societal political correctness, the members of the Live Free Movement must step up and protect private education from government mandated political correctness.

'Home schooling'

Home schooled kids test even higher than private school children. And home schooling is expanding and evolving. Parents are banding together with other parents specializing in different subjects. There are many cooperatives forming that help provide teaching aids and books. One of the biggest motivations of home school parents is to avoid the anti-God, pro-socialist indoctrination of the public school system. The number of children being home schooled is growing dramatically… and the government is scared to death. The government is trying to fight back with attempts at controlling curriculum and there is even an UN attempt to wrestle away parental control of children. But what we see again is the government fighting against the laws of nature. One of the biggest laws in the animal kingdom (humans included) is: Don't get in between a mother and her children.

One of the fatal flaws of governmental socialism is that it needs masses of under educated and morally deprived dummies to keep it afloat. But home schooled parents are churning out highly educated and morally balanced kids who will dominate over the public schoolers in the future. While the public education system does all it can to dumb down its student body, it only increases the gap of knowledge between its students and home schooled graduates. The socialist public school system is actually creating a society that will be lead and dominated by home schoolers in the future.

The concept of home schooling can be expanded. Imagine after school programs of volunteer parents teaching employability curriculums to a vast amount of disadvantaged children. Imagine a private initiative to inspire businesses to provide internships to students. These are just extensions of home schooling in that private citizens are freely passing on their knowledge to the younger generation. While many of us can't stay home with our kids and be full time teachers we can reach out and pass on our job skills a couple hours a week.

Many of you might have seen or heard commercials for a private international tutoring company called Mathnasium. They teach kids basic math skills and techniques that make math less threatening to students giving them a better understanding when they are in school and giving them improved skills they can carry with them their entire life. Imagine a similar situation that teaches kids the basics about the Constitution, capitalism, the free market and the advantages of self reliance; teaching thousands of our children information that they just won't get in the public school system. If we simply send our kids to school and figure our job is done, we shouldn't be surprised if our kids retain the moral values of their socialist teachers and professors above our own. Extending the opportunities to learn beyond the school system is good for our kids and for our nation.

Another expansion of home schooling would be an actual complete school cooperative. Whereas a private school is a business that parents hire to educate their kids, a home school cooperative would actually be owned and managed by the parents. Under this model parents could pool their recourses and rent a building, hire teachers and control the curriculum while also teaching some or all the classes drastically decreasing the per student cost while increasing the quality of education. Another innovation might be a combination of part time home schooling and part time private schooling. This model would drastically reduce tuition costs without over burdening the parent.

As the Live Free Movement expands and gains publicity, the home school and private school community will see a natural ally and quickly educate their children to take maximum advantage of a Live Free society thus creating the next generation to expand the movement. Ironically the socialists will be locked in a catch 22 situation. If they continue to dumb down their graduates, they shrink the pool of potential future socialist leaders. If they do increase the quality of education for their student body they face the prospect of many of them recognizing the superiority of living free and abandoning socialism.

'Moms; the bane of government dependency'

Education is one of the most important components of the Life Free Movement. Living Free requires self responsibility and self responsibility requires knowledge of how to thrive in today's world. To be a self reliant contributor to a free society an individual must understand economics, civics, philosophy, morality along with the specifics of their chosen profession. Within America's educational system the collapse of governmental socialism is well under way. Governmental socialism is a failure and its existence depends on the inability of its dependents to recognize its failure. Un-natural socialism can't stand up against the natural instinct of a parent to demand the very best for their children no more than it can force ants to thrive as individuals. Socialists can't fight Mother Nature. Every action the socialist education system takes to expand its power causes an equal and opposite reaction towards its destruction... but I guess if they had a better education they'd understand that concept.

Today in America there is a growing undercurrent of discontent in the public education system. Moms have had enough and the more the progressives push the harder the Moms push back. The progressives are in a hard place too. They can't outlaw non public schools because they need a place to send their own kids. Even the liberal elite know public schools suck. Public schools are great for controlling the masses but not for sending your own kids to.

The Live Free Movement needs to harness and direct the 'Angry Mom Movement' to destroy the public school system. And that job would not be very hard. Simply point moms to quality schools and give them the money to enroll their kids and they'll do the rest. The destruction of the government's involvement in the educational system is under way. If we join the battle in earnest right now our grand children will grow up not knowing that public schools ever existed.

Chapter 3

Healthcare

"The national budget must be balanced. The public debt must be reduced; the arrogance of the authorities must be moderated and controlled. Payments to foreign governments must be reduced. If the nation doesn't want to go bankrupt, people must again learn to work, instead of living on public assistance." **Marcus Tullius Cicero** (55 BC)

'Learning the hard way'

Medicare, Medicaid, the VA are all big government run healthcare programs. What do they all have in common? The all have crappy service, they all are filled with graft and corruption. They all cost way too much money and they all are going broke.

What's the solution offered by the dependency coalition? Start an even bigger socialist program that will have all the same problems just on a larger scale. To most of us it makes no sense what so ever but if your goal is not to provide quality healthcare to every American but to enslave them as welfare dependents it makes perfect sense. Healthcare accounts for one sixth of the US economy, putting it under the control of the ruling elite has been a wet dream for decades.

American socialists have been salivating at the possibility of nationalizing healthcare. If your goal is enslaving dependents then health care is the perfect vehicle. And with liberal Democrats and RINOs firmly in charge of the legislative and executive branches of the US government not much will stop them from enacting their grand scheme. But freedom lovers take heart; the game is far from over. Socialized medicine is a failed idea, that's been proved all over the world. Just because American liberals choose to ignore that fact doesn't change the reality. But as Americans just begin to live the nightmare of socialized medicine Europeans are beginning to wake up from their disasters and are now looking to privatization to bring them back from the abyss. It seems that liberals have to learn their lessons the hard way.

Since the advent of Medicaid and Medicare America has had a mixed socialist healthcare system. And during that same period we've seen tremendous problems in that system reach a boiling point. But the socialists have been unaccountable for any blame for the problems in the healthcare system because they can hide behind the private segment of American healthcare and blame it on them. But not anymore; very soon the deficiencies of socialized medicine will be laid bare for all to see. Sadly many will suffer during our grand social experiment before the casket can be nailed shut once and for all, but on the bright side, the quasi-socialist system we endure today could have survived indefinitely; the private sector propping up the social sector while the social sector drags down the private. It's important to remember that we are now seeing our future in the long term not the short term. Yes, liberals will create a huge new dependency class that they will suckle their power from for the next few decades but we're interested in changing the fundamental structure of society 65+ years into the future. Discrediting nanny state medicine might be the best thing for America.

The problem lies in the fact that when people perceive that their medical care is free they will demand more care and more expensive care. The government will not be able to collect enough taxes to cover this exploding demand and will either have to force healthcare workers to provide their services for less money or put limits on the care patients receive. If they put wage controls on doctors and medical workers many will leave the field or leave the country. If they limit care for patients they will create a nation of pissed off sick people. Most likely they will end up with what the rest of socialist Europe has, which is the worst of both scenarios. As time goes on the problem will worsen and the government will begin to reel under the weight of ever increasing healthcare costs to the point where they cry for a solution. Of course at this point conservatives will raise our hands and gently say, "Privatization"

It's funny that today we hear loudly that our healthcare system is "broken" but 45% of it is run by the government. Amazingly nobody asks if it is the government run part that is doing the damage. That question is drowned out in the mad push to have government run 100% of healthcare. Why? Because single payer healthcare is not about healthcare, it's about power for the single payer...government.

The battle cry of the left is "The uninsured, the uninsured!" but as we calculate the enormous cost of government run healthcare it would almost cost less to buy every single uninsured person a private policy. And this is not a bad place to start as we advance healthcare into the live free movement.

We've been promised that we can keep our health insurance if we like what we have. Our government just wants a "public option" to offer us one more choice. But what we'd see happen is the government would require private insurance to provide more and more benefits while they restricted their ability to raise premiums driving most insurers out of business. If they did allow private insurers to raise their rates to cover the new mandates many employers would drop their employee plans and tell their workers to go public. Sure you can keep your present coverage…what? Your present insurer isn't in business anymore? Oh well, good thing you have our public option. But the public option would suck. Americans with real ailments are not going to want to wait for 6 to 9 months to see a doctor. So they will begin to look for private insurance on their own which will be expensive. They will look for ways to reduce their premiums creating a market. That market will arise from the ashes to provide affordable and timely healthcare and the cure to today's healthcare dilemma will begin to emerge.

———————————

'Create a market and they will come'

I never had health insurance from the time I was 18 until I was 48 years old, luckily I was pretty healthy. At one point I needed two tests and my doctor lined them up at a local hospital. I was paying cash for the tests and was told they would cost $1,200. I was shocked and called my doctor and said I couldn't afford that. His nurse called around and got me the same two tests in a building 100 yards from the hospital for $120. Had I had insurance I would have gotten the expensive tests without question thus contributing to the healthcare crisis. In the Metro Detroit area there is a company that offers CT scans and MRIs for a fraction of the cost that hospitals charge. When I went to the doctor I paid cash. When he wrote me a prescription I asked if that was the cheapest meds he could prescribe. When I went to emergency I fought like hell to have other people's subsidies taken off my bill so I only paid what I fairly owed. Hard core haggling can knock 60% off an emergency bill; especially when you're both looking at the $5 Band-Aid item.

The answer to high cost health care is the responsible consumerism of the individual. Where individuals purchase their own policies and use deductibles to lower their premiums. The advantages of deductibles are twofold. One, it lowers your premium payments and two; it makes you a much better consumer of healthcare. If your initial payments come out of pocket, you are going to shop around for a good deal. At that point you will be stunned at how much price gouging is going on in the health care industry that is being covered up by insurance companies. You'd think insurance companies would want to keep costs down but they don't. They calculate their costs and add a percentage as profit. If you spend $100 and they make 5% they get $5. If you spend $1,000 they get $50. The only difference is that you premium is higher. The more expensive your healthcare is, the more profits insurance companies make.

As more and more Americans lose their employer based insurance, flee from the public option and begin to buy individual policies with high deductibles a market will emerge to offer deals to the now attentive shopping health care consumer. As this market grows it will put pressure on hospitals to compete with these new businesses and lower their costs for tests and procedures. This competition will lower the overall costs of private insurance thus attracting more people away from the crappy public option into the Live Free Movement the same way parents shun 'free' public education and pay out of pocket for private education.

This is where private IRAs, the corner stone of the Live Free Movement, comes to the rescue. You can use your private IRA to leverage and reduce your healthcare costs. It works like this: You set aside a portion of your IRA in a liquid money market account that is used as a potential deductible to reduce the cost of a private health insurance policy. If you don't use it, it stays within your account. In your twenties it may only be a thousand dollars, in your thirties it may grow to five thousand; ten thousand in your 40s, etc...

It's basically the healthcare savings accounts that George Bush originally proposed but not contingent on legislation to be defeated by leftist politicians. What George Bush didn't tell you was that you already have the legal right to open a savings account. If you personally set aside that account for your healthcare, that's your business. And you can also buy personal health insurance with a substantial deductable that would drastically reduce your premiums. All the elements already exist, what's missing is a significant movement in this direction. Corporations could also benefit by setting aside deductible savings accounts for their employees. We are already seeing large companies investing in preventative healthcare for employees to reduce their costs, setting aside deductibles would make sense.

Live Free™ could play a huge role here. By coming up with novel ideas to reduce healthcare costs and educating a huge segment of the population who begin to demand these new services a market is created and businesses will step in to satisfy that demand. For example: A program by insurance companies that assigns a specific price to a certain test, say $400 for an MRI. Then allows their customers to shop around for a lower price and then splits the difference. If a customer gets an MRI for $200 they get a $100 rebate check and the insurance company saves $100. If thousands of people are shopping around for $200 MRIs Companies will arise to supply that demand. Hospitals that charge $400 will either stop providing MRIs or lower their price. In a few years all MRIs will be $200, insurance companies would lower their MRI allowance to $200 and consumers would start shopping around for $150 MRIs.

The root of today's expensive healthcare costs is that individuals are discouraged from shopping around. If we bought TVs the same way we buy healthcare your $800 big screen TV would cost you $5,000. Another problem with government healthcare is that Medicare and Medicaid under pay for the services they request which causes many healthcare professionals to limit or even refuse service to folks on the government plans. Doctors and hospitals that do accept these programs pass on their losses to the rest of us driving up our costs. Insurance companies stay mum and pass on that cost to us in our premiums and we just assume healthcare is naturally expensive. The truth is that we are subsidizing everyone on the government dole from our taxes and our premiums. Government healthcare is a lot more expensive than any of us realize.

'Spreading the cost'

Society will always have individuals that are extremely sick who cannot afford the healthcare they need. If we accept the premise that every citizen will receive the health care they need, than as a society we need to spread that cost amongst all of us. The vast majority of illness in America today is preventable and due to the life style choices of the individual. By making healthy life style choices we can reduce the overall cost of healthcare, but having government mandate what we eat or smoke or by dictating what we can or cannot do infringes on our freedom. Private healthcare providers must be able to use our life style choices to determine our premiums. If we smoke and are overweight we should have to pay more for healthcare. This allows the market place to provide incentives for healthy living. We are not told how to live right by the government but encouraged by the private sector. Freedom also means the freedom to engage in fattening cheese burgers or cigarettes as long as you're willing to pay for it.

Of course there are people who are sick through no fault of their own and who cannot afford to pay for their healthcare. We can set up a pool to provide coverage to the uninsurable similar to pools set up for no fault auto insurance. The coverage would be paid for by taxing everyone's insurance premiums and letting the individuals in the pool pay what they can towards their premium and subsidizing the rest. Government coverage wouldn't be provided; insurance companies would compete to offer coverage knowing that the premiums would be covered through a combination of consumer payments and subsidy providing a profit to the provider regardless of the ailment.

We can even cover those who refuse to acquire health insurance by assuming that every citizen is automatically enrolled in the pool at birth. Give tax credits for all private insurance payments. Those who choose not to purchase healthcare insurance pay the pool through their taxes. If they go into an emergency room and don't pay the hospital bills the hospital gets paid from the pool. If they pay cash for their medical care it's tax deductable. Everybody pays their fair share, everybody's covered.

Socialists try to use class warfare arguments to advance their power goals. One of their ploys is to demonize the notion of profit and then demonize any company or industry they chose that strives to attain a profit. Today our leftist government is trying to demonize the health insurance business claiming that the problems within the industry are caused by bad CEOs in search of evil profits. But profit isn't evil; it is the life blood of freedom. You can solve any societal problem by making its cure profitable. If the problem in healthcare is the "uninsured", just make it profitable to insure them and someone will step up and fix the problem.

'Live Free™ *and Healthcare*'

Live Free™ can make a difference by encouraging stock brokerages to set up insurance deductibles within IRA accounts. As people move towards this approach companies will move to meet this demand. More choices and opportunities will arise for citizens to shrink their healthcare premiums. As the pool of available deductable funds for healthcare grows more companies will want in on that. They will begin to compete for this new growing segment of the population that shops around for healthcare and their biggest selling point will be cost.

Live Free™ can also help educate people as to the connection between healthcare and consumerism. Show them how ignoring the cost of overpriced procedures ultimately comes back in their premiums. Increased consumer awareness will lead to an entire industry that caters to the demands of the Live Free Movement. If a family of 4 spends $3,000 a year for insurance and decides to save a $1,000 deductable it will immediately lower their premiums, but if they shop around and buy $120 tests instead of the $1,200 tests they'd normally ignore, it will drive down costs throughout the whole industry. If you let the insurance company buy 8 tests for you it would cost them $9,600. They don't care because they are going to cover that cost in your premium; otherwise you're paying for it. If you pay $120 for 8 tests it costs you $960 out of your deductable and costs the insurance company nothing. That savings is going to drastically reduce your premium. These savings don't occur unless large numbers of people begin to become smart healthcare consumers but the Live Free Movement can help by encouraging more and more Americans to join the effort. If consumers are given more freedom to choose insurance especially by purchasing plans across state lines, competition will force insurers to pass the savings along to the growing pool of deductable holders instead of letting them subsidize a shrinking pool of non-deductable holders.

From my experience with my tests I reduced my costs by a factor of 10. But even if smart consumers could achieve a 50%

reduction it would drastically affect the cost of healthcare. If insurance premiums were halved many more could afford insurance and many more private companies could offer healthcare plans.

And private companies could benefit from deductable accounts also. For example: If a company set aside a deductable account for its employees and then asked an employee to shop around for medical care, that employee would show the company the difference between their highest and lowest quote and split the difference with the company. While this might not work in every instance and an employee might not want their employer to know what medical treatment they are receiving, it would be a powerful incentive to promote medical consumerism. And it's good for the company; they would be helping to lower their overall insurance costs and saving some money when their employees become smart shoppers. Employers might also make deals with healthcare providers to offer volume discounts to employees for common tests or yearly physicals.

It's important that the Live Free Movement introduce, support and promote these types of initiatives. As they begin to take hold and grow they will create a market and the companies that supply these policies will begin to advertise in an attempt to attract new customers. In doing so these advertisements will promote the concept of medical consumerism along with their products which will lead to a change in the culture allowing free market medical care to become the dominate accepted choice for healthcare.

'Government healthcare in the Live Free World'

Like with all our other Live Free initiatives our goal is to eliminate the government's involvement in our social programs but we also realize we need the government as a back stop and provider of last resort. If someone does fall through the cracks the government needs to be there. But in our Live Free society the goal of the federal government to create a huge enslaved dependency class will be gone and our population will be striving for personal independence. The need for massive government involvement will be gone and the pool of truly needy will be small and shrinking. At this point the wisdom of the Constitution should prevail. Let the states handle it and even when they do have them merely purchase private policies for the needy.

The role of the federal government is simple; they should set the ground rules that the healthcare system functions in. They should protect Americans against fraud and harmful medical practices while also protecting the profitability of the healthcare industry. They should objectively and aggressively enforce the laws they write but make sure those laws are fair and in the best interest of the American people not politicians. The federal government's role is to work for us; to protect us not enslave us. With states handling all social considerations and the feds none, the feds become a more credible policing force that seeks out corruption within the states; the separation between state and fed becomes functional. With the federal government micro-managing the welfare state there is nobody left to police them. That's why there is so much waste, graft and corruption in government healthcare; and why nothing but lip service is ever done about it.

We need to attack the premise that since every American has a right to healthcare that therefore government has to provide all healthcare. We don't buy into the old Soviet notion that all people have to eat therefore we must have government controlled communal farms. In America we accept that everyone must eat so the government steps in and pays for the poor to purchase privately produced food.

America has the best health care in the world because competition drives private companies to innovation for profit…yes once again profit is not evil, it is the life blood of freedom. Take any problem; make its solution profitable and you will have your solution.

So many ailments like heart disease and cancer were considered fatal 50 years ago. Today they are survivable and curable. That improvement in the human condition should not be ignored. And it was made possible by the healthy pursuit of profit. MRIs are a fraction of the cost they were 15 years ago. New is expensive but it always becomes common place and cheaper. What doesn't change is technology's impact on medical quality. As a matter of fact, as MIR machines become cheaper their quality improves the same way as HDTVs become cheaper they have more quality features. Today non-evasive robotic surgery is expensive because it's new. 10 years from now it will become common place and less expensive. With shorter hospital stays and less complications, these machines will eventually drive down medical costs.

In the single payer socialized medical world hospitals and doctors won't have to compete for income. Their income will be predetermined by the political bureaucrats. They will have no incentive to buy expensive new technology. Government bureaucrats will determine that 'new' technologies are too expensive and refuse to pay for them, never allowing them to become 'commonplace' and therefore less expensive. The success of medical equipment companies will not be determined by their innovation or their quality or cost. Their success will be determined by their political connections. In the free market, success is determined by the value of your product. In the socialist universe your success is determined by greasing the pockets of politicians, even if it means lowering the quality of your product: Thus explaining the Yugo.

The members of the Live Free Movement don't want to wait 6 months for a test while tumors grow inside them. What they'd really like is a vaccine that prevents cancer. Socialized medicine will never ever deliver that vaccine, that's only possible in the realm of free market medicine. Remember, it's socialized Europe that is rationing all the innovations invented by private America companies. When was the last time you heard of lives being saved by innovations developed in Michael Moore's beloved Cuban medical utopia?

Chapter 4

Unifying the Message

"Open discussion of many major public questions has for some time now been taboo. We can't open our mouths without being denounced as racists, misogynists, supremacists, imperialists or fascists. As for the media, they stand ready to trash anyone so designated." **Saul Bellow**

'Who are we?'

There are many great conservative organizations in America; there is also a wealth of good conservative leaders. But one problem is the lack of unity; a deterioration of the Conservative Coalition. Many of the members of separate conservative groups feel betrayed by George Bush and the Republicans who served in Congress with him. Liberals have done a great job of convincing Americans that they are one pay check away from poverty and that only the government can save them. Too many moderate Republicans are gun shy from being attacked as "mean spirited", willing to make Granny eat cat food. Instead of fighting back, these moderates have jumped on the dependency band wagon. Their motto is: "If you can't beat 'em, join 'em!" The problem stems from the fact that too many Americans see no alternative to a government provided safety net. What they see is state welfare or starvation. Conservatives have failed to provide adequate private alternatives and to promote those alternatives to convince a majority of Americans that there is a better way.

A number of steps have to be taken to undermine the welfare state. First, alternatives have to be expanded and second they have to be promoted. And in both cases a coordinated focused effort has to be made by a unified conservative movement. The job is too big to be handled by any one conservative group and infighting between conservative factions leaves no one standing to challenge the real enemy…the welfare state.

Conservatives are separating themselves from the Republican Party who they feel are betraying them and in the process they are becoming more 'radical' in the sense that they demand the immediate dismantling of the welfare state without compromise, which is an impossible demand. At the same time Republican 'moderates' seek to accommodate the vast dependency bureaucracy and 'contain' the spread of socialism but end up only alienating themselves from their conservative base. This arrangement guarantees a far left majority in the US for the foreseeable future. But the long term plan of the Live Free Movement can bring together both groups. It alleviates the fears of moderates who tremble at the thought of being considered "uncompassionate' and provides hope to conservatives who today see no relieve from a socialist onslaught. Today conservatism is divided and weak.

That's why **Live Free**™ is so important. It's an organization whose mission is conservative unity; an umbrella group that can foster communication between the many conservative factions, that can provide greater representation of conservative thought in the mass media and that can adequately battle anti-conservative prejudice throughout society.

But seeing the Live Free Movement purely on its relation to politics is a mistake. It's ironic that extremists from the left and right equally view the election of a certain type of politician as the solution to all their problems especially considering that the politician will exploit either one of them for his own personal advancement. The Live Free Movement strives to shrink government no matter who's in power and as its members begin to realize their ability to thrive without government and its membership rapidly expands, the politician will eventually come to heal, restoring the master/ faithful dog relationship meant in our Constitution. Changing our culture will force government to assimilate.

Government is very slow and intractable. A certain amount of grid lock was deliberately built into the system but our free society changes quickly and in unpredictable ways; it's always in a state of flux. Just look how quickly I-Phones and the internet change the way we communicate and socially network. In the same way we can effect social and political change by embracing the potency of our free society and giving it a true vision and ability to organize. Government can be humbled from "death by a thousand cuts". Free people can quickly undermine and counter socialist legislation before it's even passed. As long as people can see the long term advantage of fighting government oppression with a unified goal they will find new and creative ways to "cut" at the bureaucracy. Even if those cuts are small, in the thousands if not millions they will affect Washington no matter how big it grows.

A great starting point would be an annual 'Live Free Conference'. It would identify three major elements of principles for all Free people:

1. **Items we clearly agree on**. These are principles that all groups can unify behind; the initiatives and language needed to maximize the impact on society by saturating the media with an understandable concise message. Less government - personal responsibility – free market discipline - are all areas we can agree on and these shared principles need to be constantly reinforced

2. **Items we can negotiate.** These are principles that are more important to some groups than others but where groups can cover each other's backs by adopting common language that promotes our unified status. For example; an anti-abortion group and an anti-public school group might have unrelated agendas but they can both benefit and support each other by adopting the same personal responsibility language.

3. **Items we agree to disagree on**. These are principles that differing groups cannot come to terms over. It's important to develop an atmosphere where these issues can be debated and discussed without vilifying the other side. By fostering a level of respect for our commonality we can more easily tolerate our differences. And in a society where the success of our agenda relies more on an inclusive free market and less on an adversarial election system, our differing views can both be allowed to flourish letting the free market and free society decide.

Thomas Jefferson said, *"The legitimate powers of government extend to such acts only as are injurious to others. But it does me no injury for my neighbor to say there are twenty gods, or no god. It neither picks my pocket nor breaks my leg."*

In a free society differing attitudes can be tolerated because an individual can retain his opinion without oppressing or being oppressed by another's opinion. Once government attempts to legislate a solution, it must pick one opinion over the other and force both party's obedience; or worse yet, settle on a compromise that offends both opinions. Splits in the conservative coalitions become divisive because opinions are seen as eventually being legislated which will ultimately diminish somebody's freedom. When actions and plans are discussed and taken outside the government, individuals are liberated to participate or not without threat to their personal freedom. They are free to live and let live; the true root of tolerance.

The Live Free Movements mission of cultural change without legislation allows others to have their opinion without fear of losing your own. The movement is voluntary which places it under evolutionary pressure. It must perform or it will be abandoned. Live Free initiatives must pass the smell test. It must be of value to its individual members. But at the same time it will reflect its members. While organizations within the movement will make suggestions and provide opportunities, each individual member will do battle in his own way. Success will breed success and like the I-Phone or internet, independence will expand in unpredictable ways…and probably at a breath taking pace. Unity will come from shared accomplishment and that unity will spill over into the political arena.

'Politics: A side Show'

While we pursue freedom without the permission of government we must acknowledge that they can either help us free our society or more likely fight us every step of the way. We should be engaged in politics to the extent we can as long as it doesn't interfere with our main objectives. Political change should be a byproduct of the successes we achieve in the free society. When we see politics as our only salvation it amplifies small differences between people that should otherwise be working together. There is a great difference between agreeing on broad political concepts like 'smaller government' and the practical application of designing programs that realistically shrink the government. Americans nod their head in approval to the general ideas put forth by conservatives, and then they vote for the specific government bennies that the Democrat offers. So the Republican candidate wrongly concludes that he needs to offer a government benny to achieve a vote when in reality he needs to make sure no voter actually needs or wants the benny his opponent offers and more importantly convince the voter that the benny his opponent offers is harmful to his personal finances. If we end up proving through our actions that private bennies beat government bennies than the Republican will gain stature.

When Bill Bennett became President Reagan's Education Secretary he was prepared to dismantle the Education Department, but the administration saw that it would be politically damaging. What wasn't done was planting the seed of government education's private replacement by putting in place the means for America's parents to find a path to private education. Ronald Reagan was clearly able to articulate the concept of smaller government but he lacked the practical ability of implementing that ideal. Had the Reagan Administration passed two small programs that expanded the ability of private schools to compete with public schools and to begin to transfer public school operations to the states, today the idea of abolishing the Education department would be not only possible but probably expected if not complete already. And the 'No Child

Left Behind' wouldn't be a federal program; it would be an American tradition.

In his second term George W Bush expended his political clout on Social Security Reform which failed. But had he initiated a plan for the establishment of private IRAs for every child at birth and means tested S.S. for the top 5% of wage earners, S.S. reform would be taking place today all on its own.

Too many Americans are addicted to their government bennies. The mere mention of the possible elimination of a program sends fear to the addicts, and liberals are masters at spreading that fear. The approach should be to not directly threaten these programs but only plant non-threatening seeds that by the time they grow to threaten the welfare state their roots have grown firmly into the fabric of the nation. If the combination of private IRAs and S.S. means testing grows to the point of genuinely threatening the existence of S.S., it will also have grown enough to make any attempt to fight private retirement political suicide for the left. The goal is to have private retirement compete side by side on a level playing field with government retirement. Even if the government doesn't allow the playing field to be level, the superiority quality of private retirement can still win the day.

Unity of the Live Free Movement will come from its diversity. Millions of individuals taking independent and unique actions resulting in common change. Yet each individual sees a common goal…a common vision of a future dominated by maximum freedom. The unifying vision of the Live Free Movement is what's important. The small seeds have to be carefully designed. But because the tiny seed does not resemble the mighty tree it will become, the movement needs to be educated as to its importance and the patient maintenance it needs to flourish over the coming years and decades. While each free person will discover their own path, the dream has to be articulated and constantly reinforced.

The left has been very good at unifying their message. Language created by Karl Marx and his posse a hundred years ago is still potently used in the modern liberal lexicon. Liberals are masters of double speak like "Social Justice" which actually means unjustly confiscating the wealth of one person and redistributing to someone who hasn't earned it. Conservatives need to master the art of "Truthful Speak". Take the language of the left and apply its truthful meaning to deliver the conservative message allowing the general public to use its common sense to arrive at a term's true meaning. The language the left uses works great on the general public, it's just that the terminology and the left's agenda have nothing in common. It would not be hard to make job creation, private retirement and private education fit under the term of "Social Justice".

'Looking down the road'

What is needed is to promote the overall, long term vision on which particular initiatives can be measured against. How does a tax proposal help or hurt the long term goal of advancing private retirement? Would this bill hamper private school enrollment? We need the means to see the big picture; to see the destination so everyone in the boat can row together. Privatizing socialism is a huge endeavor and its different elements have to work in concert if it is to compete against and surpass government socialism. Having your private IRA support and enhance your private health care or your college tuition goals is important for your independence. Helping Americans understand and take maximum advantage of private opportunities is essential in reducing then eliminating the welfare state.

It's imperative that long term comprehensive vision of the country that thrives without government interference be created and then articulated broadly. Everyone within the movement must be able to stand up and loudly proclaim, "This is where we need to go, this is how we get there, and this is what awaits us when we arrive!" Call it "**Vision 2075**" When the left tries to attack it, be prepared to defend it and use the occasion to start a national debate. When the nation takes notice use the opportunity to bring the likeminded into the movement.

And don't think for a moment that governmental socialists won't be fighting this effort every step of the way. There has to be an entity that can counter and dispel the propaganda from the left. At each election the leftist will offer up an immediate government freebie as enticement for a vote. Offering a benefit that is 25 to 50 years out into the future is a hard sell. But by designing programs that function without a government mandate the object at first is to protect those private programs from government interference and convince Americans to take advantage of them without asking them to give anything up.

Our actions today will be small and incremental but our vision must be gigantic and all encompassing. Clearly seeing the destination allows you to take the first few steps in the right direction and allows you to travel the most direct path to your goals. Because we use many small independent groups and individuals, chaos can ensue and efforts can become counterproductive. But with a unified goal these far flung groups can move together and support each other through the journey.

In 2010 millions of Americans went to the polls to protest against the expansion of government. A huge segment of Americans can clearly see the disaster of an out of control federal bureaucracy. By having a clear articulated goal and well lit path for success, these people will begin to matter and effectively shift American culture to the freedom and independence our nation was founded on. Even those that must stay dependent on government subsidy can at least give back by providing the opportunity for freedom to their children. The millions of individuals who would make up the Live Free Movement are already there, they just need something to believe in and a vision to get there. And as the movement organizes, the spot light will be put upon them. Their sheer size will demand attention. The Left and their media shills will become fearful and try to defame them but even that negative attention will make millions more take notice. Many of them will understand the message and join the cause.

Young people can see today that Social Security will not be there for them. "IRAs for Life' will make sense and give optimism to the younger generations. As they begin to take advantage of the new opportunities we provide, they will gain a sense of hope and security and they will begin to feel about the Live Free

Movement the way the 60s generation feels about government socialism. Many of today's youth will find work in the media and will eventually shift it back to the somewhat objective institution it was meant to be. When this generation begins to have kids, they will be more engaged in rooting out socialist indoctrination from the curriculum of their kids. Unlike government socialism, living free plays to the strengths of mankind's natural instincts. The free socialist institutions we create will exist independent of the corrupting forces of government and naturally evolve in the best interests of its members or they will fade away. The day will come when the idea of the government running a socialist program will be considered ridiculous.

———————————

'Live Free™ *the nuts and bolts'*

I see **Live Free™** as a non-profit umbrella organization that inspires and promotes many other groups that harmonize their efforts while focusing in on their individual tasks. **Live Free™** would sponsor conferences amongst various groups to develop a unified message; a platform so to speak. And it would help forge ways for these various groups to combine and coordinate their message. **Live Free™** would raise money to conduct an ongoing media campaign that promotes the general principles of the movement like personal responsibility and self reliance. **Live Free**™ would also inspire the creation of many new organizations that enhance, expand and protect the Live Free Movement. These are some of the organizations I would like **Live Free**™ to create:

Live Free Rating Bureau (LFRB) - A panel that develops rating systems for various societal entities. For example; a rating system that measures the impact of legislation on the ability of individuals to live free. If legislation had a poor Live Free Rating the entire movement would be mobilized to defeat it.

Another rating would be the Consumer Live Free Rating. The **LFRB** would analyze all publicly traded companies and devise a rating that measures a combination of what a company accepts in corporate welfare and how much they spend on lobbying and donating to political campaigns. Americans who are living free need to be educated consumers and would shy away from companies that are in bed with the federal government. As the Live Free Movement grows, companies will want to tap into that market. They may even begin to advertise that they "Collect no corporate welfare: Donate to no political campaigns and last year provided 1000 private school scholarships." I imagine the day when you enter a business you see the **LFRB** sticker on the door right next to the **BBB** (Better Business Bureau) sticker.

The **LFRB** would also rate private social programs like retirement, medical insurance and education to give consumers a good idea of how to take advantage of the private programs available to them and will be able to distinguish what private programs give them the biggest bang for the buck.

Defense of States Rights Union (DSRU) - Modeled after the **ACLU** it provides legal aid to challenge the federal government whenever and where ever they step on the 10th amendment. The **DSRU** would have legal experts and lawyers who constantly confront Washington going all the way to the Supreme Court when necessary. They would have branch offices in all 50 states and work closely with them to craft state sovereignty legislation and state ballot initiatives and then coordinate those initiatives in multiple states.

American Association of Free People (AAFP) - Modeled after **AARP** it would have a membership of people living free who would get discounts from Live Free rated companies and would receive a monthly magazine that provides information on how to thrive without government interference. The **AAFP** would also use the clout of its membership to battle against anti-Live Free legislation and politicians. The AAFP would also educate their membership in how to steer clear to government entanglement and how to reduce their tax burden reducing the funds Washington needs to expand.

Leftist politicians use political activists and agitators, many from union ranks, to conduct protests and civil disobedience to basically extort booty from private companies, individuals and from government. They intimidate or bribe politicians to start or expand social programs or to fund their activist organizations. The activist organization ACORN for example was given billions of dollars in the 2009 stimulus bill which they in turn used to promote a socialist agenda and engage in actual criminal activity like voter fraud.

The **AAFP** would be able to counter these groups by monitoring them and organizing its membership to confront these groups where ever possible. If Jesse Jackson were organizing a protest to demand a payoff by some company **AAFP** could have counter protestors there to negate the effort. **AAFP** could also organize protests at places like ACORN offices to draw attention to government's collaboration in criminal behavior. At all times AAFP members would attempt to convince individuals from leftist organizations to join the Live Free Movement. Who knows, maybe Jesse Jackson himself will join the movement for the sake of his kids and their kids.

Capitalist Anti-Defamation League (CADL) This organization would challenge leftist attacks on capitalism and capitalist leaders. It would attack the double speak language of the socialist movement by constantly exposing the flaws of socialist double speak. It would bring slander and liable suits against leftist whenever possible and would use the leftists own hate speech legislation against them by pushing for capitalists and conservatives to be included as protected groups.

One of the **CADL**'s most important missions will be to root out anti-capitalism from America's education system by constantly forcing institutions, teachers and professors into court to defend their anti-capitalist dogma. The more anti-capitalist a university professor is, the more time he will spend in court and the less time he will have available to pollute his students minds in the class room. The **CALD** would push to have anti-capitalist hate speech policies enacted on college campuses. We want the political correctness movement fiercely defending the 1st amendments freedom of speech for their own sake. If they win, we win. If they lose, we win.

While these are just a few of the groups I can imagine, it's important to remember that thousands of private organization and businesses already exist that we can use to live free. A clear vision of the future will help us maximize the opportunities we already have and allow us to begin to live a life style that rejects and destroys government socialism. And as we live this life style and the financial burdens of the welfare state subside, we might be pleasantly surprised to find out that we are much more wealthy than we ever imagined when government was confiscating 50+% of our money.

'Build it and they will come'

To create **Live Free**™ it would need a leader or group of leaders. They would call together a convention that would establish a platform and an overall goal along with a path and benchmarks. Of course these tenets would be non-binding. The Live Free Movement is non-governmental and merely makes suggestions not law. The success of its plans will be determined by their accomplishment not by which politicians they were able to purchase. The first objectives would be to raise funds to attract membership from individuals, organizations and businesses that already encompass the ideals of the Live Free Movement. Ideally **Live Free**™ would try to divert funds away from political campaigns to symbolically show that the movement is all about shrinking the nanny state from outside the government regardless of party affiliation. The first initiative action taken by **Live Free**™ would be to encourage a group of prominent conservatives to convince stock brokerages to start the 'IRAs for Life' program. Of course this program would exist independent of **Live Free**™ but they could still take the credit for initiating the program and use it to show the direction of the whole movement.

I actually imagine someone like Sara Palin (if she doesn't run for president) leading **Live Free**™. The truth is that she could do more to shrink government from the outside than she could achieve as president. Even as president and especially as much hatred as the leftists in Washington have for her, she would have a hard time enacting real reform. The dependency coalition would explode at every initiative she proposed. As a matter of fact the best she would probably do as president would be to talk up the Live Free Movement from the bully pulpit. But any attempt to legislate against the welfare state will meet huge resistance from both sides of the aisle. But from the outside she could move much more freely. Big government proponents tend to focus on the government. As long as she is on the outside she will appear as less of a threat. By the time the Live Free Movement begins to alter the nanny state it will be too late. The membership of the movement will help fend off the movement's attackers.

I believe with the right leadership, a concise message and goal and with the IRAs for Life program under its belt that **Live Free**™ would quickly expand. Millions of Americans are watching helplessly as government power grows out of control and they have no idea what to do about it. **Live Free**™ is the answer and would provide a place for disaffected Americans to unite and finally feel like they can control their own destinies. **Live Free**™ would be a welcome breath of fresh air.

'Culture war: The counter offensive'

We truly are fighting a cultural war. But if a small group of intellectuals sit around discussing conservative principles amongst themselves little forward progress will occur. The concept of self reliance and rugged individualism has to be sold…marketed with a robust comprehensive vision using all the tools available throughout the global media. The media exists within the free market and there is nothing keeping conservatives out of the media except their own indifference to what they witness in today's industry.

Ronald Reagan brought individualism out of the dark because he knew exactly how to market the conservative brand. His Hollywood experience taught him how to get the most dramatic impact when delivering his message. Ronald Reagan was to words what Steven Spielberg is to action adventures. He presented self reliance as something exciting, he made us all want to be a rugged individualists. But we can't rely on one person like Ronald Reagan to carry all the water for the movement. Mass media exists and we need to learn how to use it for maximum effect.

Liberals are great at saturation marketing to promote their progressive agenda. They use code words like "Social Justice" or "fairness" which represents an entire philosophy about redistributive socialism wrapped up in a few words.....and who could be against 'social justice'? Conservatives need to speak about "Social Independence" and "Freedom from poverty". It should be automatic. When a liberal uses the term "social justice", it starts a conversation about "social independence". Liberals are also great at building coalitions; many unrelated causes covering each other's back, all using the same code words. Conservative coalitions need to unite their marketing strategies and try to tie their diverse agendas under a cohesive conservative message. The Live Free Movement naturally encompasses this within its evolution.

The objective of the Live Free Movement is to expand private alternatives to government welfare programs. These goals are met by private companies that provide a service like any other business. They want to expand and grow and they do so by advertising for new customers. The customers that they already have exist because they understand and believe in the principles of the Live Free Movement like responsibility and self reliance. It's only natural for a company servicing the Live Free community to want to espouse and promote those values. They create new customers by convincing people to adopt these principles and by making them look attractive in their advertising. We need to create the language of the Live Free Movement, as the membership of the movement grows, companies who service the demands of the movement will want to use that language (and therefore the message) that appeals to their customers. This will put the concepts of the Live Free Movement on prime time TV and lead towards the cultural change in attitude that will expand the movement.

The Live Free movement is based in truth and its tenets are primal. Advertisers who target products to males tend to appeal to man's desire to be attractive to the opposite sex. It's primal. They advertise to women to appeal to their sense of family. Again, it's primal. Appealing to the primal desires of males and females to be independent providers and nurturers is natural. Leftists tend to advance their agenda through deception and double speak. They strive for a single payer (the government) health care system but they promote it as "choice and competition" A government run system offers no competition and only one choice…the government. The Live Free Movement can attack leftist double speak with good old fashion truth.

Language is fundamental to the human species and precise language is crucial. Objective truth is the foundation to precise language. The political establishment deliberately pollutes the language with double speak and outright lies to support actions that would otherwise seem insane if articulated truthfully. But truth is a powerful weapon if applied. Socialist terminology is carefully crafted to disguise its true meaning, but by usurping the language the left adopts, flipping it over to is precise usage and then ingraining it into the language of the Live Free Movement, the language is easily recognizable to the public and the common sense of its proper usage makes it difficult for liberals to continue using the double speak definitions. Liberals are then forced to create new unfamiliar double speak terminology but again, by usurping and properly defining the language, liberal messages become difficult to get out. If liberals are forced to use accurate language to define their policies, the battle will be won.

The point is that it's not enough to just to formulate the Live Free agenda it has to be promoted extensively and new innovative ways have to be created to urge the public to stay away from government dependency. There is no reason not to use every available method within modern media. Make the self reliant, rugged individualist the hero that average Americans aspire to be and it will spread in modern advertising. The ideal of the Live Free member will become respected and will be used to sell cars, tooth paste and razors. At this point the culture will be transformed.

'Infiltrating the Left Wing Media'

If the only time you promote the conservative message is during a general election you have to compete with the freebies offered by the welfare state. And as we see with most elections they end up being dominated by name calling and negative campaigning. The conservative message always takes a back seat. If we see our goal as not winning an election but as changing the culture which would eventually lead to election wins, it opens up a whole new realm of possibilities. America's commercial media makes hundreds of millions of dollars from candidate commercials leading up to an election. But the day after the election that revenue stream dries up. That's when the conservative movement needs to step into the void and put out its message. Not attack ads against the other side but public service messages to educate the public on alternatives to government dependency and the virtues of self reliance. The major networks may be controlled by ardent socialists but they quickly turn into filthy greedy capitalists when you wave advertising revenue in their faces.

One of the mistakes of past attempts at cutting the welfare state is that untested alternatives are placed side by side with proven programs and Americans are told they have to give up one to accept the other making it easy for liberals to argue that a benefit in the hand is worth two in the bush. By designing programs that can exist alongside the welfare state and slowly erode them over time, conservatives can avoid all discussion of cutting government programs. When liberals start screaming "Cuts!" we can simply make the claim that there is no intention of cutting anything right now we are simply adding something on top of what the government offers. More not less….as a matter of fact it is the liberals that are demanding cuts; cuts in private benefits.

The Live Free Movement needs to make the claim that it is the liberals who are denying benefits to Americans.

But public service announcements are a small part. The Live free Movement needs to infiltrate every aspect of modern media, even within the content of TV shows and movies. The right does well with talk radio and Fox News is quite successful but in the rest of the media, especially in the entertainment industry, conservative thought is blocked out, even censored (Try being a conservative speaker on a college campus.). Movies are a major facet of America's cultural heritage. The old WWII movies are part of who we are as a nation. Today the Hollywood leftist culture has a death grip on the industry. For example; no positive portrayals of the Iraq war are allowed. Anti Bush and anti-military films never do well at the box office but the leftist response is that Americans are war weary and don't want to see anything about Iraq. But they've never tried a patriotic pro-American movie about Iraq, and future generations of Americans will be cheated out of their heritage because of it. Iraq has many untold battles with tremendous acts of bravery and sacrifice that would make gripping movies. In the future we might see the Iraq in a different light. This is just one example of media censorship that must be overcome.

The Live Free Movement has to be involved in financing movie projects and TV shows. And it's not about donating, it should be profitable. Personally I think a compelling pro-American war movie about Iraq would be a huge box office hit. Surely there are enough breath taking battles and acts of heroism that would entrance the movie going public. And there is no reason that conservatives shouldn't make a healthy profit by making the most of an untapped market....the pro-American movie lover. There are only so many movie theaters across America for new releases. The more spots that are taken by popular films with a positive Live Free message the less Americans will have to endure the monolithic leftist movie choices they have today. It's sad to think that if you make the American general the hero instead of the villain and the mass murdering terrorist as the villain instead of the victim that you'd be creating a fresh unique movie.

It's about how to smartly investing in Hollywood. There are conservative actors, directors and producers in the industry but their opportunities to express their beliefs are rare. The trick is to help fund conservative authors and playwrights and to invest in production companies developing pro-Live Free projects. We've seen recently pro-Christian brokerages that offer mutual funds that do not invest in companies that support pornography or abortion, there is no reason that mutual funds that feature pro-conservative investments couldn't be developed, including profitable entertainment enterprises. Live Free members would use their consumerist powers both in the media they watch and in the investments they hold.

It's also important to make inroads in the TV entertainment industry. While a glass ceiling for conservatives exists at the major networks there are ample opportunities in the cable side of TV. The major networks are already losing market share and if popular Live Free leaning programs on cable begin to further that market share loss, the networks will be forced to emulate conservative programming or go out of business.

It's ironic that most of the ardent promoters of socialism in Hollywood have bigger incomes than the evil CEOs they vilify on a daily basis. Like in Washington it's easy to advocate a culture of shared misery for the downtrodden masses when you yourself are living in the lap of luxury...and that's a common denominator of global socialism over the last century. The ruling elite never do wallow in the mud with the peons they enslave. Just imagine if the movie industry was nationalized. Actors and actresses became government employees not allowed to make over $35,000 a year. I guarantee that without exception each one would become an outspoken member of the Live Free Movement. Very seldom do you see someone advocating the nationalization of their own industry. As a matter of fact maybe a concerted effort that demands wage caps on Hollywood actors might get them to shut the hell up.

Again it's important to remember that the tenets of the Live Free Movement are primal; they'll appeal to the common sense of average people. This will allow the message to thrive throughout the media as long as the road blocks to its dissemination are broken down. And as more and more people bask in common sense they will begin to expect nothing less and begin to reject the double speak, lies and idiocy of the socialist politician.

Chapter 5

Sane-Regulation

"There's no way to rule innocent men. The only power any government has is the power to crack down on criminals. Well, when there aren't enough criminals, one makes them. One declares so many things to be a crime that it becomes impossible to live without breaking laws." **Ayn Rand**

'Defining terms'

Conservatives need to change our position on de-regulation to sane-regulation. Protecting the public from harm and fraud is a legitimate function of the government. Football's a great game, but it has a league that sets down the rules and there are referees to enforce them. But you never see the refs go into the huddle, call the plays then take a hand off and head for the end zone. Our government wants to get in and play the game when it needs to be strictly a referee. Government needs to macro manage not micro manage. In our antipathy towards government, conservatives push for de-regulation, but the left has effectively defined de-regulation as allowing 'Corporate America' to rip off the public. During the 2008 financial crisis Democrats were quite aptly able to blame de-regulation as the culprit when the real crime was Congresses' political meddling that did the most harm. We need to redefine the argument. The term **'Sane-Regulation'** needs to be a buzz word that describes the concept of – *'seriously enforced rules of conduct to protect the public interest combined with sensitivity towards protecting free market competitiveness.'*

Sane-regulation should protect the people from fraudulent products and unsavory business practices, but it should also protect the health of the economy that the people rely on for their livelihood. It needs to look for ways to assist business to be more efficient and competitive while it watches over them, and it must maintain the level playing field that individual businesses depend of to be prosperous. And just as important, sane regulation needs to protect legitimate businesses from the predatory practices of the socialist politician.

The problem with having the government enter the game as a player is that at some point it has to pick a side. Of course businesses rightly decide that they must make an attempt to influence this new player to remain competitive so they divert their attention from their industry towards politics. As businesses begin to heavily invest in political campaigns trying to purchase a sympathetic government ally, the politician responds by doling out either corporate welfare or punitive regulation to increase his worth to his new suitors without regard to its overall economic impact. The politician's campaign chest takes precedence over the jobs of average citizens. And every penny the business diverts to purchase a politician has to be paid for by its customers or employees.

This incestuous relationship results in a set of regulations that poison the natural balance of supply and demand that a healthy economy relies on. The 2008 housing bubble is a perfect example of political pollution harming the free market. Government politicians threatened and seduced the banking community into providing subprime home loans to people who were not qualified to pay them back. Adding these new unqualified buyers into the housing market increased demand which drove up property prices and created an un-natural force to balance the market with expanded supply. It was clear to many in the banking industry that eventually this bubble would burst so they attempted to mitigate their risk by bundling these bad loans into derivative commercial paper and reselling it where it spread throughout the economy. Again, these toxic assets could have been sanely regulated but corruption in the political/business relationship barred common sense reform to protect the fortunes of political donors while throwing the general public to the wolves. To add insult to injury, after the crash, the very politicians who were at the heart of this economic calamity smugly sat on their thrones wielding blame at everyone else except themselves for the worse economic downturn since the late 70s...one of them became president. Had there been an adequate separation between economy and state and an inkling of sane regulation the 2008 collapse would have never happened.

A capitalist economy is cyclical. It has ups and downs but our knowledge of macro economics has grown tremendously. The technology exists to drastically ease the impact of economic downturns, but the will doesn't exist. That's because those in charge of making the effective and timely adjustments to the economy have perverted motives towards the nation's economic health. What is Washington's biggest priority; economic growth or class warfare? One of the main components of sane-regulation needs to be protecting the free market from the meddling of self serving politicians. Too often politicians will pass legislation to curry favor from a certain special interest group while ignoring its impact on private citizens or businesses. We need agencies that work as a buffer and develop regulations that meet the goals of protecting the public and free markets. Let Congress provide oversight but tame their desires and ability to micro manage the economy; thus the separation of economy and state.

One of the biggest tools socialists use to advance their cause is class warfare. They have been brilliant in demonizing businesses and corporations as a societal evil. But if "social justice" is to be defined as eliminating poverty than the free market delivers more social justice than the government could ever dream. Businesses not only deliver income well above the poverty level to the vast majority of Americans, they also provide the wealth the government uses to pay their dependents. It's the free market that provides all the country's social justice; it's the government that is shamelessly glorifying itself from the hard work of other people.

Sadly too many politicians are elected using class warfare propaganda and after taking office they write legislation designed to punish wealth creators as a means of backing up their anti-capitalist propaganda. The Live Free Movement needs a long term battle plan to combat class warfare dogma. And sane-regulation is an important tool for the right. Conservatives must always have intelligent alternative legislation to counter the left's anti free market rhetoric. Again, it's not enough just to espouse lofty principles; concrete actionable proposals need to be on the table. Much of the class warfare argument is promoting the notion that the rich got that way by cheating the poor. Sane-regulation can be used to dispel this distrust and as the government's welfare burdens decrease they can shift their priorities to enforcement of regulations thus creating less crime and more trust.

If conservatives have a future vision of America in 2075 they can write the legislation today that will lead us down the path to that specific goal. We must always ask, "How does this advance the cause of privatization?" "What needs to be in place today to reach our goals decades in the future?" "How does this specific legislation affect the overall economy and the laws of supply and demand?"

If the health of private social programs is to be dependent on the overall health of the free economy then it's important that careful management of our regulatory systems be essential. We've seen that the bursting of the .com bubble and the collapse of the housing bubble caused tremendous harm to our economy putting strains on people's private IRAs and 401Ks not to mention their jobs. But both of these bubble bursts were completely predictable. Unfortunately short sighted political motivations kept responsible regulation from circumventing two avoidable recessions.

One example would be an **Economic Trends Agency** that would watch for problems in the economy like unhealthy bubbles and report to Congress with sane solutions. The collapse of the housing industry in 2007 was predicted and warned of in 2001, but no mechanism existed to bring it to a level to be acted upon. An Economic Trends Agency might have had the clout to force Congress to write sane regulations to address the looming subprime mortgage fiasco long before it melted down.

As the burden of social spending gradually shifts from the government to the free market citizens who depend on those social services will want to elect politicians who will best assist the free market to increase the quality and reduce the cost of those services. At that point the election of the politician becomes dependent on shrinking not increasing government social spending, and the best way to do that is expand the economy to reduce the demand from citizens for government help. At that point sane-regulation becomes critical to the politician because an economic downturn would increase demand for spending and threaten his re-election.

'Is Corporate America evil?'

One of the cornerstones of modern socialism is to convince you that capitalism is evil. While the left gives quite a lot of lip service to fighting racial bigotry, even where none exists, it deliberately fosters hatred and resentment towards the wealthy…not through ignorance which is the root of most prejudice, but for pure political gain. Ironically they call the rich greedy while they satisfy their own greedy ambitions. They use deliberate stereotyping of the wealthy to foster class hatred but it is the wealth creators that provide 100% of the standard of living Americans enjoy today.

And a little bit of common sense goes along way here. Which represents evil more, running a business that employs people and provides products and services people want even if you make a reasonable profit, or using the coercive force of government to enslave generations of people just to expand your own personal power? It seems pretty clear but the socialist slave masters have convinced over 50 percent of Americans that the rich are evil. I wonder if a socialist politician who slanders Corporate America to get elected and then passes legislation that harms the corporation (which harms the livelihoods of the corporation's work force); does the politician's propaganda rise to the level of hate speech?

It's important to understand the history and motivation behind the slander socialists engage in against capitalism. A corporation has as its first priority earning a profit for its stock holders (which in a privatized nation means all of us); therefore a corporation has to make decisions to maintain profitability. A socialist makes the claim that the corporation's first priority is to its workers and its community and disregards profits as a worthwhile concern. This leads the socialist to be able to place burdens on the corporation eliminating its profit and when the corporation relocates to a place where it can return to profitability, the socialist claims the corporation is evil because it harmed the workers and community it left behind. While the socialist benefits by acquiring votes from the use of his convoluted logic, his argument still remains false at its core. An absolute truth remain; corporations first priority is profitability not community service. Community service is a byproduct of a business's pursuit of profit. The socialist's claim otherwise doesn't change the truth it just masks it. Decisions must be made on a basis of truth. If false conclusions are made and then acted upon, then the actions will be wrong. For example: You are bit by a poisonous snake. (Which is true) You assume you have a cold. (Which is false) You take Nyquil instead of anti-venom and you die. You based your action on flawed logic and since actions have consequences you suffered.

If we set aside the socialist false propaganda we can construct a series of truthful and reasonable assumptions, and then draw proper conclusions. For example: a) a corporation's first priority is profitability. b) Workers and the community benefit from the existence of a corporation. Conclusion: Workers and the community have a vested interest in the profitability of a corporation. That sounds overly simplistic but you must realize that that chain of logic does not exist in leftist propaganda.

Here's another logic chain: a) a corporation's first priority is profitability. b) Workers and the community benefit from the existence of a corporation. c) Some actions taken by corporations in the pursuit of profitability can be unsafe and harmful to the community. Conclusion: The community should regulate corporations to prevent harm to the community, but do so in a way that strives to maintain a corporation's profitability. (The exact definition of sane-regulation).

In America today we have a government that acquires its power from the distortion of the truth regarding our economic system and our society as a whole. Because the truth is hidden behind false propaganda, regulations based on this false propaganda are doomed to fail and are actually harmful to the nation. If we are to build a secure social benefit culture dependent on the private sector, our regulatory system must be based on absolute truth. If false socialist propaganda is allowed to poison the process we run the grave risk of enacting harmful law based on lies and doomed to failure. The biggest threat to private social programs is economic downturns; therefore we must be completely honest about what is happening in the economy so that our actions to avert or diminish a downturn are effective.

Corporations are not evil but you must understand their true nature. They exist to make a profit. Profit isn't evil. It's what we all want after we pay our bills; some left over cash. Vilifying innocent people and then stealing their money just because they've benefited by working hard and working smart; now that's evil.

Let's run another logic chain based on absolute truths: a) Politicians will be writing our regulations. B) Politicians lie. Conclusion: we're screwed. This is where America really needs to face the truth. We need to have regulations written on our behalf but we cannot trust that any politician will put our best interests ahead of their own. Today Americans elect their leaders based on what they say during the campaign and how those words make us feel with a total disregard as to whether they are true or not. After the election we find out more often than not that the words we heard during the campaign were false and we become angry that we were lied to. But don't we have some responsibility to investigate the words and determine their truthfulness before we vote for a candidate? If a candidate offers massive new socialist spending, tax cuts and deficit reduction wouldn't a little simple math exercise prove those proposals false?

It is possible for us to create institutions to filter and vet the statements of politicians before they can convert them into harmful law. And we can create agencies that examine truthfulness and possible negative effects of legislation before they are enacted. I know we have truth in advertising laws for private businesses on TV. The reasoning is that false product claims are considered fraud and could harm the consumer. But in politics making false claims is considered protected political free speech. But if a politician makes a false claim and then enacts legislation that is harmful, doesn't society have a right to be protected against this fraud? Of course, if we had truth in campaigning laws, candidates would spend the entire election season in court. So we are still left with our dilemma: We need our laws based on truth and those who write our laws are liars.

'A Nation of Laws'

The United States does not have a king who makes arbitrary decisions, we are a nation of laws that even our most powerful leaders are expected to obey. But our national leaders have developed methods to write laws that benefit themselves without regard to the rest of us. As we've seen in proposed healthcare legislation and cap and trade legislation, the scam goes like this: Have special interest groups write massive 2000 page bills with Orwellian double speak titles that benefit the ruling elite. Write it in convoluted legalese that even the legislators themselves cannot understand. Then have Congress pass these behemoth bills within 72 hours before anybody can read them and understand their real intent. It's only after the bills become law that average citizens begin to learn that they have been had, but by this time it's too late…it's the law.

The process for enacting laws set up by our founding fathers was meant to be painfully slow and difficult. The reason was that our founders knew that legislation was meant for the benefit of the citizens not for the sole benefit of the politician and that proposed laws needed to face a gauntlet of debate and criticism throughout the land. This was to ensure that only the most beneficial laws would see the light of day and that bad law would be exposed and buried. Recently we've seen with Obamacare, politicians trying to sneak through legislation with trickery and stealth that is opposed by 75% of the American people. The sad part is that these politicians actually feel they are doing their duty. Our limited republic has been corrupted and the American people must share in the blame for letting things get this bad. We've elected representatives based on the free stuff they give us without regard of the freedom they take away from us. We've allowed special interests from the left and right to bastardize our Congress for their own personal gain over the good of the nation. We've failed to limit our limited republic. Having congress write a national healthcare bill is unconstitutional. It's an area reserved under the Tenth Amendment for the states. Having Washington write that legislation without our consent and against our will is immoral and bordering on illegal.

In a free society the ideal is to have the least amount of law possible. The people follow these laws because they are deemed fair and righteous and the population has respect for the law. When the law is exploited for the benefit of undeserving special interests the general population loses respect for the law and begins to look for ways to circumvent them. The government is obligated to enforce bad law against a resentful citizenry and a police state emerges. Americans are very generous and when people are in need we rise to the challenge to help out. But our government has decided to steal money from one segment of society and give it to others who are clearly undeserving. This builds resentment from those being robbed. One of the most insidious aspects of class warfare propaganda is to convince the recipients of government charity that they are the "victims" of the very people who provide the charity they survive on. They feel entitled to their handout and actually feel animosity and resentment towards the very people their stipend was stolen from. The wealth creator resents the welfare recipient and the welfare recipient resents the wealth creator. Neither one recognizes that it is the politician who has abused and exploited both for his own personal gain. And that is the real purpose of class warfare hatred; to shield the politician from deserved scrutiny.

We are a nation of laws but law is a double edged sword; it can either protect us or enslave us. To reiterate Ayn Rand's quote at the beginning of this chapter, *"There's no way to rule innocent men. The only power any government has is the power to crack down on criminals. Well, when there aren't enough criminals, one makes them. One declares so many things to be a crime that it becomes impossible to live without breaking laws."* The socialist politician through regulation attempts to control every aspect of our lives leaving us with only two choices; obey his excessive laws or be deemed a criminal giving the state the right to punish the law breaker. Within the national healthcare bill is a provision that requires you to purchase insurance by law. This means if you decide to pay cash for your medical treatment out of your own pocket you are a criminal subject to prosecution. In essence your freedom is removed and replaced by enslavement to a far away politician who will decide what medical care you can receive and when you can receive it. I believe our founding fathers are rolling in their graves right now. The fact that every American is not at the steps of the Capitol with torches and pitch forks shows the insidious way socialism creeps into our lives over the generations until we wake up one day to realize we have no freedom left. But our salvation lies in the fact that the politician can't take our freedom without our consent and we can regain any freedom we have lost. Any law can be repealed and we do have inalienable rights that exist above the reach of politicians. When our Founding Fathers spoke of inalienable rights in the Declaration of Independence they weren't writing law that could later be withdrawn or overturned, they were declaring a fact that these rights exist beyond government and beyond regulation and cannot be taken away but only voluntarily surrendered. Because of this fact all our rights are recoverable. Of course our founders envisioned in the second amendment that this might require the use of force and tried to give to future Americans the ability to conduct civil war or armed rebellion against an oppressive government but the Live Free Movement is a way to do so without bloodshed.

Yes we are a nation of laws but laws can be repealed, our right to live free cannot. While we strive to live apart from government we must also be good custodians of our government and leave a sound body of law that assists future generations to live free. And beyond the law, our society needs to abide by a voluntary code of conduct…a set of morals. While it's paramount that we show tolerance towards those who chose a different life style, it's equally important that a level of courtesy and respect be afforded to the interactions of all people. The counter culture mores of civil disobedience and "in your face" confrontation from the 60s needs to be replaced with good old fashion civility; maximum personal freedom with ridged but voluntary politeness. These ideals can't and shouldn't be legislated but they should be demanded and promoted throughout society. This concept can only be upheld when all of us are willing to speak out whenever we see incivility whether in the media or on the streets. You want to protest? Sure, go ahead. Just be polite about it.

Chapter 6

Federalism

"The Tenth Amendment is the foundation of the Constitution" Thomas **Jefferson**

'Our Constitution had it right'

Our nation gained its independence from England as 13 colonies each having the potential to be an independent nation. The United States was original constructed with a weak central government to ensure the independence of the individual colonies but united toward a common defense. But the weakness of our central government posed serious problems not at least is being able to raise an adequate national defense. So we went back to the table and wrote our Constitution.

From the beginning our founders realized that governmental power was dangerous but governmental weakness was also dangerous. They used as their guiding principle the concept of *checks and balances*. This allowed a government entity to achieve the power it needed to fulfill its duty but provided a competing entity to check and limit that power. This is written all throughout the Constitution. We easily recognize the principle when we think of the separation between the three branches of government, the executive, legislative and judicial branches. But there is also the separation of power between the citizen and the politician; elections. And between the government and the press as encompassed in the first amendment of the Constitution.

But what is often overlooked is the separation between our federal and state governments. The Founding Fathers knew that a weak national government was bad but they also knew they needed the states to check an over powerful central government thus the need for balance as in the *balance of power*.

If you remove the politics and study the concept of checks and balances and the separation of power on their own merit, to the individual of any political persuasion with the desire for personal freedom, they're just damn good ideas. It's obvious that our nation is out of balance. Our states are too weak.

Our federal government has reached the point where it is deliberately exasperating and perpetuating our nation's social problems to advance its own thirst for expanded power. Our states have an obligation…no a duty to assert the power that the constitution mandates for them. The states are required to check the power of the central government. The truth is there are multitudes of ways for our states to battle back if we would just realize that not only can we, but we are supposed to. The 10th Amendment was not some afterthought; it was put into the constitution for a reason. In the words of Thomas Jefferson, *"The Tenth Amendment is the foundation of the Constitution."*

'Slaying the big monster with 50 little ones'

Most conservatives agree that Washington's giant welfare state is not in the Constitution. The Constitution doesn't say anything about what individual states can provide, but it does say that whatever it is, it's the states that should provide it. State government can be a vital bridge between the transitions from federal welfare to private welfare.

Politicians propose social programs to entice the general public into believing that they intend to fix a social problem. But the reality is that the hidden goal of the federal politician is to create dependency by building a bureaucracy. Not only do the people who collect direct assistance from the program become dependent, but so do all the people who have jobs administering the program. The politician gains power by coercing the votes of all the people collecting and administrating the program he's created. They've also been able to make the states dependent by confiscating the wealth of their citizens through income taxes and then forcing the states into submission to get that money back in the form of block grants.

Our federal government is so bogged down in the minutia of micro managing the administration of social programs that it strains the resources that should be dedicated to the fed's primary role, which is as protector of individual rights and guardian of the home land. When large federal programs turn out to be wasteful, ineffective or downright counterproductive they can't be eliminated. The problem lies in the fact that they haven't been created to solve the problems they claim to address, they're veiled purpose is to create bureaucracies. Protecting the bureaucracy takes precedence over eliminating a needless wasteful program. And no one can do anything about it. There is no means for American citizens to directly write law on a national level. The process is filtered through the ruling elite. Our nation was designed as a republic where the majority could not directly abuse the minority. Our elected representatives are supposed to be a filter to lessen the chances of an abusive majority and our state governments were supposed to check the abuses from our federal representatives who in turn would keep a sharp eye on our state governments.

While we can debate how our leaders "evolved" the Constitution around the limitations that were intended for the federal government, we must remember that just because they did it doesn't mean it was the right thing to do. It was a mistake and we can clearly see today the ramifications of that mistake in the loss of our liberty and the loss of our hard earned money. The original Constitution had it right and just because there is case law established that was able to bastardize the Constitution doesn't change that fact. Just because there is case law doesn't mean we throw our hands up and say, "Oh well, nothing we can do now" The smart thing to do is to return and strengthen the original intent of the Constitution and demand that the trickery used to side step the intent of the constitution be reversed.

The politicians in Washington won't want to give up their power and will fight to keep it, but as individuals we are not powerless. Today we've seen 36 states pass non-binding resolutions in an attempt to reassert their sovereignty over the intrusion of the federal government. While these resolutions are unenforceable they clearly show an interest in state governments to roll back the power of the federal government and show that the desire to engage Washington is growing. What's missing is sound legal initiatives and adequate organization to attack the feds.

It's important to remember that are state politicians are well...politicians. They want power just as badly as the national guys do. While our long term goal is to limit the power of all politicians, in this instance "The enemy of my enemy is my friend". A temporary alliance between free people and state politicians would be very useful.

There are a number of ways the Live Free Movement can use their states to battle the feds. The most important is to fix the social issues the feds rely on to amass power. Healthcare, education, poverty, the environment, transportation, these are all issues the federal government uses to seize power. By not just addressing but solving these issues at the state level we castrate the federal politician. Another battle tactic is to unify states to coordinate attacks against the federal government. As earlier stated, 36 states have passed non binding states rights resolutions. If those same states passed a unified resolution it would send a powerful message. Another plan would be to educate the population to elect federal politicians based on their loyalty to the state over their loyalty to a national Party. The goal of the national Parties is to usurp the Constitutional rights of the states. But federal politicians are ultimately elected by the citizens of an individual state. If loyalty to the state becomes a major campaign issue, political hopefuls will have to address the issue. A federal congress that puts the needs of their state above the desires of the UN is good for America.

While none of these are a magical pill that solves things over night, alone and together they begin to shift the culture. And that is our goal. Prosperity in the states, loyalty to the states and power to the states returns America to a point of balance. No matter what political persuasion you adhere to, solving social issues is what you want. Whether left wing or right wing, ending poverty is what you desire. Left wing gets social justice, right wing gets higher profits, and hard working Americans get more money in their pockets for their families; the poor get a higher standard of living and hope in the future.

And in the future when the federal monster is finally tamed we may fear the power accumulated by our state politicians but don't fret. We do have a weapon to use against them; the state ballot initiative.

'The Equalizer: State Ballot Initiatives'

One weapon that free people have at the state level to fight state politicians and more importantly; to control state politicians is the ballot initiative. With state ballot initiatives people can directly write law and bypass the politician. The ballot initiative is the equalizer; the weapon that the average citizen uses to effectively battle the greed of the state politician and his dependent minions. If states ran their own social programs the citizens of that state could make clear choices. Chose either a program designed to empower a politician but one that exasperates a social problem or a plan that actually fixes the problem.

With the ballot initiatives social issues can be attacked head on. Within a state, average citizens can directly address issues of poverty, education, transportation, healthcare, retirement, unemployment, etc… and make meaningful change. Of course the socialists will battle back with their secret weapon, the courts, like we've seen in California, but with every blatant abuse of judicial power the momentum of change grows. If an initiative is over turned put it on the ballot again and again. Make a politician's election contingent on his support of the initiative and a transformation of the judiciary that rejects it instead of being based on the goodies he hands out. Within a state, issues can be much more focused and Live Free citizens can attack on multiple fronts. Concepts can be honed and proven within states and good ideas will spread to other states eventually gaining national attention and the pressure for national change.

We can invent many new tactics for attacking the feds, get them on ballot initiatives, pass them and watch the feathers fly. And initiatives don't have to get passed to be effective. Say a group of people start a proposal to make it illegal for federal IRS agents to operate within a state's borders. It would be very popular and surely get the signatures required to get on the ballot. And if it were allowed on the ballot and passed it would surely be disqualified by the courts. But just the gall of slapping at the federal government would bring untold number into the federalist cause. California has passed a number of ballot initiatives on taxes, immigration and gay marriage that have been over turned by the courts. But they are not lost causes. They are warning shots across the bow of the ruling elite letting them know that regulating against the popular will is a dangerous endeavor.

And the ballot initiative is not the only tool for the Live Free Movement. Look, politicians love power. State politicians love power just as much as the Washington gang does. And controlling huge budgets and their bureaucracies means power. It's a matter of convincing our state legislatures that they might be able to get their hands on some of those federal dollars and like typical politicians they'll start to salivate. As individuals it's much easier to control our state governments then the federal government. Let the state devour the feds then we devour the state.

There are many creative initiatives that could gain popular support:

- Forcing a shift of state funding of public schools into parent controlled private school vouchers

- Demanding adult education or job training to receive welfare payments.

- Requiring an annual state's rights conference that invites other states to coordinate efforts to roll back unconstitutional federal welfare programs.

- Expand tax deductible charities that target poverty while diverting tax money from the IRS to state based social solutions.

- Crafting healthcare regulation to motivate private over public insurance.

- Tort reform.

Even when ballot initiatives fail or are over turned by the courts they still stimulate a debate. And if the Live Free Movement is able to get out the message of self reliance, personal responsibility and privatization it works to change the culture. It's important to remember that the Live Free Movement is about more than laws; it's about changing the culture and promoting self reliance and personal responsibility. Ballot initiatives can advance community standards and promote Live Free mores. Initiatives that look for private over public solutions should put the message of personal responsibility within the bill's language. It also provides an opportunity to make it profitable for private companies that directly address social needs to thrive and level the playing field making private companies able to compete directly with wasteful government programs. Win or lose, if an initiative has the language of personal responsibility it directly challenges PC speak that promotes victimology and irresponsibility. It encourages more and more people to stand up and say "the emperor has no clothes"

While our goal is to reduce government involvement at all levels, state government does have a role where bigger infrastructure projects need larger supervision. And regional cooperation between states as opposed to federal control should be considered. And a weaning process will need to occur. First transferring socialism to the states then shrinking it at the state level. In an atmosphere where the culture looks privately first and only turns to government where the cost and logistics are blatantly obvious, free citizens can use state government constructively but must always be vigilant to keep it limited and to keep the feds out. But even when state supervision is needed it's important to limit their involvement to an oversight roll while letting the private sector do the actual work.

One must remember that ballot initiatives are purely democratic and can be abused with the majority exploiting the minority. Again the balance of power comes to play. State constitutions help protect individual rights but our Federal Constitution grants us certain "unalienable rights" that state laws must adhere to. In a free America, enforcing the US Constitution and our individual rights should be the most important focus of the federal government. Our founding documents were carefully designed to balance and diminish corruptive government power and pit state against national as a means to keep both limited and honest. It also checks the power of the majority against the individual. We live today in an age of imbalance and this folly is evident.

'Getting Started'

Education is a logical starting point. Socialized education is in shambles and is despised throughout the population. Even poor people (the socialist's meat and potatoes dependency block) are crying out to get their kids into decent schools. Public schools, especially in poorer neighborhoods are appalling bordering on the criminally negligent. A poor person might vote to expand or maintain his government handout but rich or poor, parents want their children to have a better life. The Live Free Movement can tap into this rift between politician and dependent but first we must understand that relationship between the national socialist structure and its dependents if we are to intervene on behalf of the poor.

The philosophy behind Sol Alinski's "Rules for Radicals" is to organize the underprivileged to demand government benefits. This is the "community organizing" that we hear Barak Obama tout as his tool to gain his personal political power. It combines groups like unions and government welfare employees to help recruit poor people with the promise of payment of money you earned, which was confiscated from you through taxes. Political groups like Moveon.org and other non profits raise campaign money for left wing politicians from all the members of the leftist coalition. Remember most of these people are receiving their income directly or indirectly from the government. In essence they are paying kick back money to the politician from money that was stolen from you. In extreme socialist cities like Chicago or Detroit even people working in the free market are hampered by intense government regulation and interference forcing them to pay tribute to the politician to conduct business. People like Jesse Jackson and Al Sharpton and groups like ACORN assemble mobs that extort money from legitimate businesses with the threat of boycott or violence and again some of this money is funneled back into the war chests of the politician. In return for funding the politician's campaign and bringing bodies (alive or dead) to the polls on Election Day, the politician repays the members of the coalition with money taken from you.

On the other end the leftist politician uses oppressive regulation and corporate welfare as a 'carrot and stick' approach to extort money from American business. The tribute money paid by these businesses or excessive regulation lowers their profitability and ends up lowering the wages of their employees or increasing the cost of their products. Again this money is taken from our pockets. In the worst case scenario a business will just relocate to another country lowering the availability of jobs and increasing the pool of poor people willing to vote for a socialist in exchange for a government handout...again, your money.

But the Live Free Movement can organize too. But instead of using kick backs we use freedom and prosperity as the oil to grease the machine. If the goal is to eliminate poverty then free people have to unite with the poor and work together to help them out of poverty. Education is an ideal starting point. Live Free members would united with the poor to pass a ballot initiative to divert state education funds into vouchers to massively expand private education for the poor breaking the back of the welfare machine. All the funding of the welfare state one way or the other comes from the pockets of people who work in the free market. When a government dependent becomes a free market wage earner, his relationship with the machine changes. He transforms from being a politician's ally to becoming prey, and his priority shifts from milking someone else's pay check to protecting his own.

Education is unique because it addresses the welfare problem from multiple angles. Being a wage earner creates a much higher standard of living than being a government dependent. This is a powerful incentive for recruitment to our side. Education is the door that allows one to enter this higher standard of living, that's why the public school establishment is so concerned with replacing real education with diversity education to try to enslave the children of its present dependents. And while dependents are willing to promote and protect the welfare state for themselves, they don't want that life for their children. This is the opening we need. We want better education for the children of the poor and so do they.

Within most communities there are groups of people who want educational reform and choice. The worse the public school system the greater the support for reform. While many of these people might be part of the welfare coalition, with this one particular issue they are at odds with the socialists and they can expect no cooperation from the leftist machine. They stand diametrically opposed to the powerful public school lobby and the socialist goal of 'dumbing down' the dependents. The Live Free Movement needs to seek out and unite with these groups and attempt to reach out to poor parents to split in half the decades old leftist machinery.

The idea is to use the ballot initiative to design an educational agenda that pulls people away from poverty and therefore government bennies and to get poor parents engaged in ensuring their children live their lives as productive workers in the free market. For example:

- An initiative that offers school vouchers to the lowest income students at first, targeting the most likely to receive aid in the future. This would force the state to divert its funds to expand the private school system while shrinking the public school system and reducing the amount of welfare demand in the future.

- Mandate a job skills curriculum percentage for all schools in the state. Strive for maximum employability from all future graduates. Replace anti-capitalist courses with basic economics.

- Create unfunded IRA and college accounts for all children in the state and provide incentive for citizens to donate and invest in these accounts.

- Allow tax credits to parents who send their kids to private schools freeing them from the unfair burden of paying for private and public schools at the same time.

- Force public schools of compete for funds directly from parents based purely on performance and not on political favoritism.

In Michigan they use the proceeds from the state lottery to help finance the public schools. It might be very possible to use the ballot initiative to divert those funds towards private school vouchers allowing the citizens to do an end run around the public school teachers unions.

With the ballot initiative voters can also impact the state's curriculum. If a state has a problem with a segment of its population that is chronically unemployed due to under education, it may decide to look at its schools and reduce the level of its political correctness curriculum and replace it with more job skills education benefiting the average citizen. In a decade or two that state would be graduating employable citizens with more citizens paying taxes and less collecting benefits. Citizens can force federal programs into extinction by eliminating poverty through "community organizing" leaving them with no one to collect a benefit.

The Live Free Movement can play a vital role in transforming education. And because the lack of education is a root cause of poverty, reform sets in motion an irreversible trend towards self reliance by creating a population with the knowledge and wisdom to choose a Live Free existence. As free people begin to build in numbers they are able to place on the ballot and then pass other serious reforms. Imagine a state that has a Live Free majority of voters, and they in turn enact long term policies that reduce poverty, increase wealth and drastically shrink the size and scope of government interference. They will be a beacon for other states trapped in their own socialist nightmare. The Live Free Movement will use success in Free states to promote the movement in others. As the transition spreads from state to state and personal social responsibility expands the call to limit the federal government will escalate along with the combined political power of the Free states and its citizens.

'The Transformation'

One positive aspect of federalism is the competition between states and the ability of average citizens to move to different states to take advantage of the government that state offers. One state like Michigan might decide to be the Mecca of socialism while another state like Tennessee decides to be the sweet heart of entrepreneurs. People who want to collect welfare can move to Michigan while people who want to work can move to Tennessee. We've already been watching this migration take place for the last 30 years. What many socialist leaning states have learned is that a socialist system cannot sustain itself without feeding off the wealth created by entrepreneurs and business. If the wealth creators are abused they'll just pack up and leave taking their capital and wealth with them. The state with the highest standard of living, the lowest taxes and the least social problems will attract more businesses and individuals. Fixing social problems would be a benefit to a state, where as the feds want to expand poverty to acquire dependents.

For decades Michigan was able to expand its government socialism on the back of the automotive industry. But they've crossed over the 'wealth creator to dependent' golden ratio and have forced their wealth creators to flee the state. Since the state can't actually create wealth, they can only steal it; they now don't have the ability to fund their welfare programs. Worse, the dependents they've created can't comprehend that money doesn't grow on trees and will not accept cuts in their freebies. Michigan's politicians are pulling their hair out trying to figure out how to get more money out of a rapidly shrinking pool of "rich people" but can't even grasp the concept of shrinking the size of government. It's ironic: Michigan offered massive tax breaks to the movie industry and liberal Hollywood flocked to Michigan to take advantage of the chance to acquire evil profits. But it never dawned on Michigan's socialists that offering the opportunity for profit to all the planet's capitalists would create the same results. Michigan is a looming train wreck that would be fun to watch if it weren't for the suffering it will cause to its citizens. Worthless state IOUs don't buy food or pay bills. Michigan is fertile ground for the Live Free Movement.

Sadly, Michigan's dependency class will not give up easily. Corporations that pursue profit are evil. CEOs are to be publicly flogged not wooed with tax cuts. Jobs are a right even if a business has to operate at a loss to provide them. And actually having to do work while at work is considered a sign of capitalist oppression. Michigan has swallowed the class warfare propaganda hook line and sinker. But even within this state dominated by the left is a huge population of free people looking for a solution; people who would embrace the Live Free Movement. Michigan is on the verge of collapse but it also has the opportunity to be a Phoenix rising from the ashes.

States crumbling under socialist failure can come back by joining the Live Free Movement, maybe not officially but they can create an environment where it is easier for its citizens to live free. A state with low taxes, common sense regulations and a small welfare burden is going to attract jobs and jobs are the life blood of the Live Free Movement. States that create this environment have a competitive edge over other states and these other states will want to emulate their successes. As more and more states begin to Live Free they become strong enough to reject the welfare demands of the federal government.

A transformation of a state like Michigan from a welfare basket case to a vibrant free market Mecca would launch the movement to new heights and provide a powerful argument against a century of leftist propaganda. The transformation of just one state could change the whole game. Success will breed success. An influx of business to the new Live Free state will come mostly from wealth creators fleeing other collapsing welfare states and help create a domino effect. The citizens of failing states will look to the success of the new Live Free state as a possible solution to their woes. If the Live Free Movement is robustly in place and plays a leading role in the transformation a single state it allows the movement to promote its long term goals and its cultural changing philosophy. Providing a clear cut set of directions, a functioning apparatus for grass roots "community organizing" and a shining example of success could make the movement formidable in failing states all over the country. As living free becomes the goal of a majority of America's states, they will naturally turn on Washington's massive welfare bureaucracy and demand relief.

'How do we fight back?'

I imagine **Live Free**^{TM} starting an organization modeled after the ACLU; let's call it the **Defense of States Rights Union**

(DSRU) a non-profit group that battles the overreach of the federal government at all levels. It would be a national organization with volunteer legal experts and have 50 branches at the state level. The organization would:

- Challenge in court all federal legislation that steps on the Tenth Amendment.
- Come to the legal aid of individuals, businesses and states that had a dispute with federal over reach
- Initiate and support state ballot initiatives that are designed to challenge federal power.
- Coordinate multi state efforts to roll back federal over reach.
- Help states coordinate new social programs that chip away at the federal bureaucracy.

A unified unrelenting demand for the enforcement of the Tenth Amendment should be an obsession for conservatives. Every rule, regulation and penny collected by the federal government should be challenged in court for its constitutionality in regards to the 10th amendment. Transportation, education and many other examples of federal meddling would provide fertile ground for confrontation. High profile court cases would start a national debate on States Rights and federal overreach.

A good starting point would be to chip away at the federal government's involvement in transportation. Have **Live Free**™ start an advertising campaign that educates the public on how they could save money by not having to pay for big federal mass transit political boondoggles, and instead have their state divert that money into actually maintaining the roads. And there is nothing stopping states from joining together to oversee larger regional projects if those projects overlap between states.

The advertising campaign would go like this; "We can't fix that pot hole in front of your home in Kansas because your tax money is being sent to Seattle to build a light rail system that no one will use." The truth is that the demand for light rail projects throughout America doesn't exist. If that demand did exist and the potential for profit existed then surely the private sector would be willing to step in and take advantage of the money to be made.

States could refuse to directly use federal block grant money on highway projects. Take the money offered in the block grants and deposit it in a permanent endowment. In the future when the federal government gets out of the transportation business, states would then have a continuing source of road funds to offset their citizen's tax obligation. Putting federal transportation block grants into endowments would be an embarrassment to the federal government and be a potent symbol of federal overreach. At some point the federal government would try to restrict these endowments which would set up a battle over the fed's role in local transportation. If the feds try to deny a state their share of transportation funds the state should go to the Supreme Court to argue that its citizens should have a corresponding decrease in their federal tax obligation. In the mean time states would be wise to squirrel away as many funds as it can. Once the endowment is established states would quickly realize their value. Over time an endowment could grow where a state would have a permanent source of funds for road work without raising taxes.

Where the **DSRU** can make a huge difference is in promoting a cohesive states rights agenda and uniting the states to take their sovereignty issues all the way to the Supreme Court. Again, it is important to see into the future and envision what a healthy balance of power between the states and feds would look like. Having a thought out, concrete plan for shifting federal responsibilities back to the states and being able to articulate the damages caused by abandoning the 10th Amendment today is crucial. Court decisions need to work well 65 years from now when government returns to being "limited".

The **DSRU** could promote an annual "States Rights Conference" to unify states in their efforts to battle Washington. And this could easily become a subject of a ballot initiative that requires the state government to participate in both the conference and in completing many of the unified objectives from the conference. Once the "healthcare" debate subsides, the "state's rights" debate needs to move to the forefront

---

'Who pays taxes?'

"Soak the rich!" The battle cry for the class warrior. The reality is that all taxes eventually get passed on to the little guy in the end. A company pays taxes. It spreads that cost into the price of their product. You buy that product for a higher price; therefore you just paid that big company's taxes. The class warrior fooled you into thinking you stuck it to the big guy but it's your butt that's sore. If government spending was so justified and righteous why not just collect it from you directly? Why hide it? The government is always finding creative ways to tax you without you knowing. Why is that? The reality is they have to hide it. If you actually knew how much of your money goes to the government your congressmen's life would be in grave danger. Everything you do or touch is taxed in some way or other and most is done in away to keep you from knowing it. If they could, they'd tax the air you breathe…oh wait a minute, they're going to do that too. It's called "Cap and Trade". You will not accept them taxing the oxygen you inhale but they figure you're stupid enough to pay for the CO2 you exhale.

One of the biggest challenges of the Live Free Movement will be to educate the public and dispel the class warfare propaganda of the last century. Making the average citizen realize that "Soaking the rich!" means "Soaking yourself!" is crucial. Changing this culturally absurd notion will be difficult but it is necessary. Taxes collected by the federal government lessens the ability of your state government to address social issues and all taxes lessen your ability to provide for your own social needs and to, as a consumer, lessen poverty overall through job creation. One way or the other government confiscates 50% of your income which forces you to seek a government hand out (with strings attached) which you could buy yourself if you had the other half of your paycheck back.

One of the difficulties of states weaning themselves of the federal teat is that if the state refuses to use federal money, their citizens are still paying taxes to Washington anyway. Socialist states in perpetual financial crisis have to accept every penny they can from the federal government to balance the current year's books without any regard to the long term health of the state or the strings the feds attach to returning the money stolen from the state in the first place. During the transition from socialism to freedom states will have to endure a period of paying federal taxes without accepting federal bennies. But this transformation period can be made up for by the expansion of free enterprise. Other states regardless of the level of socialism have the same federal tax burden, so a state with lower taxes becomes attractive to business. Lowering social benefits while also lowering taxes will create a deafening outcry from the socialist apparatus: "Unfair! Unfair!" will be heard from every corner of the leftist machine. This is where the Live Free Movement needs to step up in two important ways. First, they must counter the shrill cries from the left. Use every opportunity to respond with a clear message of self reliance. "You want your welfare benefit? But your welfare state just collapsed under its own weight. You have no choice, you better become self reliant." Second, in an environment of shrinking government benefits and an expanding job market the incentive to leave government dependency and enter the work force grows. The Live Free Movement needs to be engaged in helping the dependents make this transition.

States will have to be creative to overcome the tax out to tax in gap until the free market balances their books. One temporary solution is to take block grants offered by the feds and put them into annuities. This allows the states to accept federal money while still protesting Washington's overreach. While not accepting the conditions Washington puts on the money it sends to the states might result in a denial of those funds it sets up a perfect opportunity for states to "take it to court". Even with unsuccessful court cases it creates massive advertisement for the unfairness of Washington's grasp on a state's Constitutional right to provide for its own welfare. Our long term goal is to convince all Americans that self reliance is superior to government dependency. Every opportunity to state that message is important. Americans hate taxes but they also love taxing people they hate, but if they think they are getting screwed by the IRS they are more inclined to become active and become potential future members of the Live Free Movement.

'Know Thine Enemy'

Washington DC only takes up 10 square miles. The dependents that fuel their power structure live within the borders of our states…on our turf. Cut their welfare chains and the balance of power shifts. And it's not enough just to transfer the welfare game to the states, even though in the beginning that process will be useful; it's about eliminating the dependents any politician

177

looks to exploit. The leftists that occupy Washington today have honed their game plan for decades. They build dependent coalitions and set them loose to prey on the rest of us. But because their dependents live among us, in our states, we have access to them and we have the ability to influence them and in reality, rescue them.

The socialists set traps. They use fear as bait. "Sign up for our program or go without." They never offer the better option, "Work hard and buy your own superior program." And they are not afraid to blatantly lie to us. They claim that if we don't support their socialist healthcare takeover we will be without healthcare. Never mind the fact that 85% of Americans already have healthcare insurance and the ones getting the lowest quality are the ones already on government healthcare. We know what the socialists believe and how the plan to advance their cause. Karl Marx wrote it all down over a hundred years ago. We know how they plan to advance socialism here in America. Little has changed since FDR except for the level of infiltration of socialism into our society. We know where they are; in our government, in our big cities, in our schools, in Hollywood. We know exactly how they'll react to what we do; we even know the exact words they'll use before they speak them.

We also know that they don't have a clue about who we are. They can't comprehend our beliefs or our motivations. They are bewildered about our desire for freedom and our longing for self fulfillment through hard work and personal responsibility. They think conservatives are either evil CEOs out to rape the planet for sport or toothless mountain people living in shacks without running water. Either way they view us with contempt and arrogance and consider us unworthy of study.

As we set out to reclaim our nation we must always be aware of how the opposition will react and that won't be very hard. We must be prepared to counter every move they make and use their predictability against them. If they boycott a Live Free company we need to overwhelm that company with new business. If ACORN sends a mob to protest a business we should be prepared to send a mob to the ACORN office. Every liberal protest should be met with a counter protest. Every word uttered by a leftist should be vigorously countered. Socialist double speak needs to be seen as an opportunity to spread the Live Free message. Double speak vs. common sense; few Americans will be able to ignore the side by side comparison. No challenge should go unmet.

The socialist views the world in terms of an ever expanding central government. They aren't prepared for an assault at the state level. They know how to attack the National Republican Party but attacking a state is a whole different ball game, especially a state that is reducing poverty and expanding prosperity beyond anything the liberal could imagine. And who knows, maybe someday the Republican Party will gain the wisdom to adopt the philosophy of the Live Free Movement. One thing for sure is that the day will come when a politician of any persuasion that seeks what little limited power is left in Washington will have to pay homage to the Live Free Movement to get it.

Chapter 7

Socialism

"The Founding Fathers knew a government can't control the economy without controlling people. And they knew when a government sets out to do that, it must use force and coercion to achieve its purpose. So we have come to a time for choosing" **Ronald Reagan** (1964)

'Socialism is great if I don't have to join the collective'

Socialism fundamentally means a select community pooling its recourses and sharing them equally among its members. There have been socialist entities since the beginning of mankind; the family, the tribe. Today we have a vast array of socialist units; community groups, churches, knitting clubs; people bound together for the good of the collective. These socialist units have one thing in common, they are voluntary. Members can come and go without the threat of persecution or prosecution. They are there because it benefits them. Governmental socialism is flawed because it is forced at the end of a gun. If you choose to not support a government social entity by not paying taxes for it they will come to confiscate your house. If you lock yourself in your house they will use force to take you out of your house. If you resist they will kill you or imprison you.

Nongovernmental socialism has to function through the natural evolutionary reality of 'survival of the fittest'. If a bowling team or a credit union or family unit does not satisfy the wants and desires of its members, those members are free to leave the collective. The collective must evolve or face extinction. Forced governmental socialism does not face this process of natural selection. This allows flawed, counter-productive and outright harmful programs to exist in perpetuity regardless to the damage it causes its members, the people who pay for them and society as a whole.

The principle of self reliance and responsibility is a human trait that has thrived for tens of thousands of years: It's proven. But human history also reveals a deep rooted tradition of collectivism, first to the family then to the tribe or community; but always voluntary. To Live Free is to draw on our natural instincts honed by thousands of years of evolution to flourish. And voluntary socialism is a fundamental component: Thousands of collectives working together for the benefit of their members without government coercion or interference. While mankind is intelligent and is capable of creating alternative lifestyles and making them work, there is absolutely no reason to abandon our natural character. It's arrogant for government socialists to step in and discard untold generations of evolution on an unproven behavioral model. Socialists can construct if they wish a voluntary communal model then try to attract and keep members based on the quality of their system while allowing the natural Live Free society to exist side by side as long as it's voluntary. If their system has merit it will survive and thrive. But it is unjust to force free individuals at the end of a gun to participate in an unnatural, unproven and potentially dangerous evolutionary experiment.

Many liberals point to the tribes of the American Indian as a model of socialism to aspire to. But again this model is voluntary. In pre-European America individuals could leave a tribe at will. The model that more closely reflects America's brand of socialism is the pre 1990 Soviet Union. While the roots of modern government forced socialism goes back much further, realistically the model we see menacing the world today was conceived more than a century ago in Marxist ideology. While

Marxism has been clothed in the language of "the advancement of humanity" its purpose from its inception is the enslavement of the masses. Much is expressed about the responsibilities the masses are expected to adhere to in the socialist utopia, the part about using brute force to impose that adherence and the fact that a ruling elite will impose those responsibilities is glossed over. In the classic forced governmental socialist model wealth is expected to be distributed evenly with the ruling elite exempting themselves from that formula. What are not examined are the disincentives to wealth creation that always leads to a shrinking pool of wealth available to be distributed evenly. In the end the masses end up living near poverty while the ruling elite live in opulence. The ruling elite's disconnect from the hardships of the masses hinders reform...at least until the masses show up on their doorsteps with pitchforks determined to string them up in the town square.

In America today we see the ruling elite use direct fraud and deception to enact their slave agenda through the exploitation of class warfare. The formula is simple: Remove basic economic education from the masses, demonize the minority of wealthy, bribe the majority of less wealthy to vote for the confiscation of the wealth of the minority, addict the majority to the wealth of someone else. Eventually the wealth that drives this scheme always runs out, but by that time the masses are enslaved and forced without recourse to except the diminishing resources the ruling elite grant them. We see this process taking place in America today. The wealth of America is being systematically confiscated and disbursed to the masses who are gleefully voting for their own enslavement.

'Private vs. Public Solutions'

We have many different concerns as a society that we easily see as social problems. Besides poverty, whose solution we associate with big government, we also have problems like auto accidents that are a legitimate social concern. But we seem quite willing to manage auto accidents ourselves through the private sector. There is nothing inherently wrong with a social program. An Alstate Insurance policy is a private social program. Auto accidents kill and injure more Americans and create more financial losses than poverty does, yet we have no problem letting the free market solve the issues brought on by auto accidents.

As a matter of fact the free market eliminates the vast majority of poverty in the US with jobs. While politicians give lofty speeches about how businesses need to "Pay Their Fair Share" they forget to mention that businesses do more for the social fabric of the nation than government ever could. Not only do they provide income through jobs to the majority of Americans, they provide the funding for the incomes that government offers. It's government that isn't doing its fair share by allowing the free market to eliminate even more poverty.

Social needs exist. A social program that addresses a social need and efficiently solves it or prevents it is a good thing. A dilemma arises when the purpose of a social program becomes to empower a politician above fixing a problem. At that point the program becomes a parasite. It feeds off society without returning a corresponding benefit. Because an uber-powerful politician is not a societal necessity, the parasitical program he presents that offers poorer quality at higher expense is unjustifiable. And worse it creates a bigger problem by interfering with the resolution of the social need it is supposed to be addressing by diverting funds away from more efficient private solutions.

Parasitical Socialism exists because it is able to disguise itself as legitimately addressing issues that would otherwise be abandoned. Scare tactics are used to convince people that they would suffer without their faulty program. To battle this, conservatives must begin to educate the public on the superior quality of the private alternatives and to work to level the playing field so that government programs don't interfere with the availability of those private alternatives.

To battle the government parasites we need two elements. One: a trustworthy and dependable accounting of the problem. Two: programs that have measurable impact on the problem at hand. The class warfare battle is based on disinformation provided by the ruling elite. They over state the extent of the problem they want to address and then conceal the results of the program they implemented to rectify the problem. For example: "Great Society" programs were implemented in the 1960s advertising to end poverty as we know it. Yet here in 2009 poverty is worse even though spending for these programs has been expanded exponentially. The programs of the Great society were never intended to solve poverty; they were intended to enslave individuals.

If we are to defeat the welfare state we must have the truth about the extent of poverty and we must be able adequately measure the success or failure of the actions we implement. And the government cannot be trusted to provide this information. It has already proven its motivations are corrupt and its information fraudulent. This is one of the crucial jobs of **Live Free**™. If we are to invest our hard earned money towards the elimination of poverty, it is vital that the organizations we donate to cure the problem not perpetuate them. At the same time precise, accurate and independent information will be essential to counter the false information propagandized by the left.

'Socialism vs. Logic'

One way to check the worthiness of an idea is to take it to its fullest conclusion and see if it holds up. If we use this method to compare the socialist welfare state against the free market we reveal truths about both. For example: Imagine every American becoming a welfare dependent who relied on a government check for survival. The problem is, while government can print money, it doesn't create wealth. It can only confiscate and redistribute it. If every American were on welfare we'd all starve because the money we receive would be worthless. On the other hand, if every single American were a productive wealth creator; a contributing member of the free market the entire population would thrive. By using this little exercise it can be determined that it is superior as an individual to be a productive member of the private capitalist system than to be a government dependent of a forced socialist economy.

That's the catch 22 of the welfare state. While the welfare state seeks to expand its bureaucracy by enrolling new dependents, it still is dependent itself on wealth creators for its survival. It's a high wire act trying to balance those two contradictory objectives. And no one knows where to draw the line. Too many dependents and not enough wealth creators and the house of cards topples. But to the liberal running for election the math is simple; keep your dependents enslaved at as near the poverty line as possible so that one wealth creator can finance 10, 20 or even 100 dependents. Give up the one vote of the wealth creator in exchange for the multiple votes of the dependents. Of course this set up is not in the best interest of the wealth creator or the dependents but who gives a damn? The elitist politician is in office, the rest of you can go to hell! And that is exactly the attitude the politician has towards you. They don't give a damn about you or your family or your future or your children's future. Just for a moment consider the pain, hardship and ruined lives our present economic collapse has caused and seriously consider if this wasn't a deliberate crisis to satisfy the greed and power lust of Washington politicians.

Right now in America our socialist leadership is attempting to debase the American dollar by printing them to the extent that they lose all their value. It was Vladimir Lenin who said, *"The surest way to destroy a nation is to debauch its currency."* He also said, *"The way to crush the bourgeoisie is to grind them between the millstones of taxation and inflation."* It was Alan Greenspan who said, *"In the absence of the gold standard, there is no way to protect savings from confiscation through inflation. ... This is the shabby secret of the welfare statists' tirades against gold. Deficit spending is simply a scheme for the confiscation of wealth. Gold stands in the way of this insidious process. It stands as a protector of property rights. If one grasps this, one has no difficulty in understanding the statists' antagonism toward the gold standard."* Have we witnessed since 2009 an all out attack to destroy America's economy and its wealth? Have we seen a deliberate destruction of the nation's housing market and the intentional collapse of the stock market? Two places Americans hold their saving dedicated to their independence from government enslavement. Americans were forced into homelessness; many were ruined.

The government needs dollars as payola to all the new dependents they are acquiring. The fact that those dollars will buy less food for the dependents is irrelevant to the politician; long time societal good is sacrificed for immediate political gain. In 1957 you could take a pure silver US quarter to the store and purchase a loaf of bread. Today that pure silver quarter is worth $3.50 which will buy you a loaf of bread, not because it is a quarter but because it is pure silver. In 1875 a $20 pure US gold coin would purchase a very expensive man's suit. Today that same gold piece is worth $1,000 which will still buy a very expensive man's suit. The problem is that you will never see a welfare dependent being paid in gold or silver, they will be paid in paper dollars. Without a proper economic education the average government dependent will see increases in the amount of the paper dollars they receive as a benefit but will not understand that overall, the purchasing power of those dollars will be decreasing. The deceptive nature of an increase of devalued dollars will attract more dependents who will falsely assume they are signing up for extra free money. At the same time the so called rich (including foreign governments and investors) will be diverting their wealth away from US dollars and into more value retaining commodities and currencies thus exasperating the devaluation of the dollar. In the end the socialist cycle is complete. A population of enslaved dependents living in poverty overseen by an elite ruling class insulated from the hardships imposed on their serfs.

A huge segment of Americans lost nearly 50% of the equity in their homes and 50% of the equity in their 401Ks and IRAs. If this collapse was premeditated it ranks as a crime against humanity. Lenin was talking about destroying economies a century ago as a means of radical socialist change. Is this the "change" Barak Obama spoke of so often? We do know that politicians like Barney Frank, Chris Dodd and yes Barak Obama were up to their eyeballs in demanding the massive expansion of subprime loans that directly led to the collapse of the housing market which led to the devastation of the world's financial industry. Now I find it alarming that in December of 2009 Barney Frank tries to sneak a bill in on a Friday night that calls for the government takeover of the same financial industry that he helped destroy. Personally I think there should be a criminal investigation.

We don't know if it's possible to prove that the subprime debacle was a premeditated scam but we can logically conclude that whether through negligence, recklessness or downright criminal maliciousness, the Washington politician has way too much power over the essence of our personal freedom; our private property and our financial security. Regardless of their intent, just the mere fact that they had the power to cause such extreme destruction has to be dealt with. When you add in the intimidation of the nation's automobile industry, the government power grab of America's energy through Cap and Trade and the nationalization of our healthcare system, any sane person needs to examine whether this is a concerted effort planned for a very long time; the subprime scandal makes it criminal. If you go back and research the roots of socialism from Lenin/ Marx through Alinski's "Rules for Radicals" which inspired the "Cloward-

Piven Strategy" that calls for collapsing America's economy by overwhelming the welfare state. Obama said himself, "*If you look at the victories and failures of the civil rights movement and its litigation strategy in the court. I think where it succeeded was to invest formal rights in previously dispossessed peoples, so that now I would have the right to vote. I would now be able to sit at the lunch counter and order as long as I could pay for it I'd be okay. But, the Supreme Court never ventured into the issues of* **redistribution of wealth**, *and of more basic issues such as political and economic justice in the society. To that extent, as radical as I think people try to characterize the Warren Court, it wasn't that radical. It didn't break free from the essential constraints that were placed by the founding fathers in the Constitution, at least as its been interpreted and Warren Court interpreted in the same way, that generally the* **Constitution is a charter of negative liberties**. *Says what the states can't do to you. Says what the Federal government can't do to you, but it doesn't say what the Federal government or State government must do on your behalf, and that hasn't shifted and one of the, I think, the tragedies of the civil rights movement was because the civil rights movement became so court focused I think there was a tendency to lose track of the political and community organizing and activities on the ground that are able to put together the actual coalitions of powers through which you bring about* **redistributive change**. *In some ways we still suffer from* *that. "* It's imperative that we understand what he is saying because it gives insight into how he is governing. The word "redistribution" means taking your money against your will and giving it to someone who has created no wealth. Our Constitution was carefully designed with the purpose of limiting government's role to protecting our individual freedom. The fact that the President of the United States sees the Constitution he took an oath to uphold is a "charter of negative liberties" is chilling. He complains the Supreme Court didn't *"break away from the restraints the founding fathers placed in the Constitution"* The Supreme Courts only role is to 'uphold' the Constitution. To do otherwise is well…unconstitutional.

At some point an individual that relishes his freedom and who loves his country and believes in the wisdom of the original intent of the Constitution has to make some logical choices. The socialist grab for power we are witnessing today seems formidable but the truth is it is fragile. It deeply depends on apathy and ignorance from the American people. So the question you logically need to ask your self is, "Do I educate myself, get involved and fight back, or do I ignore the problem and pretend that what I'm seeing is not really happening. Many Americans choose apathy because the idea of them alone taking on the 'New World Order' seems impossible so they choose what they can do…which is to turn the football game back on. This is where the

Live Free Movement shines. When an individual comes to the conclusion that they must get involved if they have a powerful organization to join they begin to realize that they can make a difference. Millions of Americans are outraged but they don't know what to do. Many grassroots groups like the Tea Party groups and the 912 moms are springing up but while they are making a difference, their lack of unity and direction are minimizing their potential power.

I think it is just logical to assume that when all American believers in freedom unite under a common cause, a common set of objectives and a common game plan, there would not much anyone could do to derail that train.

'Disrupting the Socialist Game Plan'

While the philosophy of the Live Free Movement is to enact change from outside the government through cultural advancement, the government as constructed in the original intent of the US Constitution is still an important component of America's Live Free future. This creates a quandary. Today's US government is a hindrance and a threat to the futures of free people but these same people still need a government to properly run a Live Free society in the future, and creating a new separate government apart from the existing one is impractical. The logical course of action is to reform our present government but that seems like a daunting task. But the reality is that the pursuit of the Live Free agenda will cause natural reform in Washington with very little effort.

There is no point where too many wealth creators become a problem in America. As a matter of fact a nation of 100% wealth creators is the goal. But there is a tipping point against the welfare state. As more Americans leave dependency and become wealth creators they create jobs which steal more dependents from the government. At a certain point wealth creating voters begin to outnumber government dependents and the elitist politician has to rethink his election campaign. Instead of pandering to the desires of more freebies for the dependents he'll have to offer plans to make the free market operate more efficiently and help the wealth creators keep their wealth....like offering less freebies to the dependents.

The Live Free Movement at its core is about transforming individuals from government dependents into free wealth creators. The destruction of the socialist power base (dependents) is just a natural byproduct of the Live Free process and the reformation of the US government is the natural outcome created by the destruction of the socialist power base. Of course the socialist will fight back but the size of the Live Free Movement itself creates its own power base to fight back. It's ironic; the Live Free Movement is actually a 'voluntary' socialist entity. Using our voluntary socialism to destroy their coerced socialism is sweet justice.

Today as we watch Washington apply Lenin's tactic of destroying the currency to deliberately expand poverty to recruit dependents it seems counter intuitive that we would be able to steal dependents in this atmosphere, but the Live Free Movement can break this cycle. **Live Free**™ will offer up ways for average free Americans to disinvest in the US dollar and retain wealth in commodities, property and foreign currencies while paying taxes in devalued dollars. As the dollar continues to decline, government dependents will see a loss in their purchasing power and their stipend will lose its value. Many will chose to leave this system for better value in the private economy. Devaluating the currency as a means of change is a double edged sword. While the socialist politician may attract potential dependents he leaves his present dependents susceptible to Live Free recruitment. If the Live Free Movement helps its membership conduct commerce without dollars while paying taxes in dollars the socialists get damaged by their own tactic. And this is not the first time this has happened. During the reign of Nero, Emperor of the Roman Empire nearly 2000 years ago he tried to devalue the currency but shrinking the size of coins or reducing the silver or gold content. This resulted in what's called *Gresham's Law* ("bad money drives out good"). Roman citizens horded older coins and paid their taxes with newer devalued coins resulting in a net loss of revenue to Rome's coffers.

It's important to understand that paper dollars have no real value except to represent economic activity. If you make $10 an hour and you purchase a pound of commodity for $10 the reality is that 1 hour of work = 1 pound of commodity. If the currency is devalued and the commodity now costs $20 but now you make $20 per hour the relationship between 1 hour of work equaling 1 pound of commodity remains unchanged. The problem occurs when the cost of commodities out paces the increase in wages. When that occurs the socialist politician benefits. But if the collective Live Free Movement can intervene and promote either direct barter or alternative currencies it breaks the cycle and will actually threaten the socialist by destabilizing his dependents who still have to survive using devalued dollars. Also if free people conduct their commerce in non-dollars and then pay their taxes in devalued dollars they end up giving themselves a tax break. It would be possible for the Live Free Movement to set up a private exchange making it easy for free people to conduct business with a variety of foreign currencies or commodities. When the day does come that Washington decides to return to a policy of financial sanity, as a nation we might decide it would be advantageous to repay a huge portion of our national debt in devalued dollars before we strengthen our currency.

As the Live Free Movement grows its members will naturally be better educated in basic economics and the importance of a culture based on self reliance and as the welfare state declines the politician who desires to cater to the Live Free vote will offer more fiscally responsible policies that begin to restore the dollar's value. But in the meantime if socialist continue to devalue the dollar, free Americans can still thrive by using barter and alternative currencies. While liberal socialists pursue a policy of high debt, rapid inflation and the punishment of wealth creation, all Americans, free people and dependents, will suffer the effects. Punishing wealth creators will just shrink the overall pool of wealth in the nation to be redistributed while at the same time the government does its utmost to recruit new dependents. Regardless of the arbitrary amount of paper dollars they give to each dependent their purchasing power will dramatically decline. Many of America's dependent class are deliberately kept near the poverty level and as the value of their handout decreases many will dip below. Of course this will be touted by the liberal as a crisis that demands immediate attention (the predictable solution being to tax someone else's money) but this abuse of the wealth creator will only lead to even less wealth to redistribute. Actions taken by the government towards the economy always have a reaction, liberals like to use the term "blowback" when referring to CIA actions but that term applies here too. By properly managing the "blowback" from leftist actions the Live Free movement can minimize the actions while maximizing in our favor the impact of the reaction. If the socialist politician punishes the wealth creator it motivates them to look for opportunities to generate wealth outside the reach of Washington which reduces the wealth available to redistribute. The Live Free Movement needs to promote these opportunities. With every little zig they enact we counter with a giant zag.

The truth is that we already know that the progressive socialist establishment will pull out all the stops to attack the Live Free Movement. We know every tactic they will use. We know how they'll protest and where they will protest and who they'll send out to conduct the protest. We know the language they will use down to the last word; as a matter of fact, we could write their speeches for them and they wouldn't know the difference. And we'll use this knowledge to frustrate them at every turn. They'll use Orwellian double speak and we'll commandeer that language and apply its truthful meaning. People hear an attractive sound bite and remember it but they seldom understand the convoluted logic the leftist applies to its Orwellian definition, but when we usurp the terminology and apply our truthful common sense definition the average citizen will understand the term and its meaning. If the liberal continues to use the term he will be reinforcing our cause. "Social Justice" will mean jobs in the free market not government welfare. Americans, and for that matter all humans, respect truth and common sense. The Live Free Movement is founded on truth and common sense, unlike global socialism, we don't have to revert to double speak, lies and deception to advance our cause. As we steal the language of the left they will be forced to create new double speak terminology but to the general public their new slogans will be unfamiliar and require some thought. But unlike the past, the new leftist double speak will be aggressively challenged. If the phrase is appealing it will be usurped with its genuine meaning into the Live Free lexicon; if it is ridiculous it will be used to discredit and humiliate the leftists who use it.

Elitist government forced socialism has been trudging around the globe for 100 years. Nothing they say or do is new. Every move they make or even contemplate is already written down in dusty decades old books in libraries all over the world. They are totally predictable. This is their Achilles' heel.

'Winning Hearts and Minds'

At the beginning of this chapter we talked about the difference between forced socialism compared to voluntary socialism. The pure definition of socialism is that individuals unite their efforts for the overall good of the collective. In the theoretical, this ultimately works to the benefit of the individual bringing the ideal full circle. We must understand that politicians are not real socialists even though we refer to them that way. They operate purely for their own self interest without any regard for the collective. The politician views the collective as something to be exploited. He forces individuals into the collective against their will with the coercive force of government even if it is unbeneficial to the individual, which also leaves the collective weaker by forcing it to accommodate unwilling members who are fighting to destroy the collective. The politician forces a situation where both the individual and the collective are damaged with the only person deriving benefit being the politician.

But we must remember that there are many people who believe in a true form of socialism. The problem lies in the propaganda of the global socialist movement of the last century. In a healthy capitalist society a free individual with protected property rights is able to accumulate the level of wealth that allows him to dwarf the level of power the elitist politician can acquire forcing the politician to be a servant of the individual. Our Constitution was intended to allow the individual to acquire any level of wealth as long as they did not infringe on the rights of another individual and America's politicians were always expected to never rise above the level of servant. The Constitution also defends the right of free association which allows the formation of voluntary social units that can generate their own wealth for the benefit of the collective. But the politician is not satisfied with being a servant; he covets the position of master. By using anti-capitalist and class warfare propaganda and wrapping it in the language of socialism, the elitist politician learned he could unite the masses to confiscate the wealth of the prosperous through the power of government and gain his master status. Those that desire and could actually achieve the benefits of being a member of a socialist entity were unable to distinguish between voluntary and forced socialism and strived for forced socialism without recognizing is inherent flaws and its exploitation by the ruling elite.

Today if we can recognize the difference between a rank and file socialist and a political elitist we can find opportunity to drive a wedge between the Kings and their armies. Remember the Live free Movement is itself a voluntary socialist entity. We need to ally ourselves with America's rank and file socialists. What we need to promote is the **Free Collective Movement**. If we can convince true socialists that the politician is exploiting them (and there is ample evidence to prove the point) and that building their collectives in a free society without government interference can help them achieve the utopia they have so long dreamed of, we can strip the politician of their power base.

The rank and file leftist has been taught by the politician to hate private capitalist insurance companies. They demand a government run single payer healthcare insurance system for the sole purpose of denying profit to any insurance CEO. And the campaigning politician promised they would have a single payer system. But now that the politician has gained the position he was seeking he has reneged on his promise. That's because he knows that non leftist Americans will boot him out of office if he does. His priority is not to satisfy the collective that he conned into voting for him but to protect his own personal position. His priority list is quite simple, first: Politician. Last: Constituency.

We can make headway here by pointing out that government healthcare may not be the right answer for the dedicated socialist. How about a non-government non-profit healthcare cooperative? They can design a system that doesn't give a penny to an evil CEO and it can be anything they want. They won't have to worry about making any compromises with those nasty Republicans.

The taming of the far left non-elite requires two main elements. One; educating them as to how wealth creation flows through the economy and how they can access that wealth without the use of government and how their bigotry of wealth creators like all bigotry is based in ignorance. And two; that politicians are corrupt and why they are corrupt and how they are exploiting genuine socialists and actually denying them the collectives they so desperately seek. Even collectivists need to eat to survive and it takes wealth to produce and deliver that food to the collective. Kill the capitalist and the collectivist dies with him.

Money flows. People are not evil because they are rich and because someone is wealthy isn't the reason someone else is poor. If a rich person invests his money it creates jobs and allows someone else to feed his family. If a rich person puts his money in the bank the bank loans the money so someone else can buy a car which allows an auto worker to feed his family. If a rich person buys an opulent yacht the worker who built the yacht feeds his family. The grocer that provides the food in turn can feed his family. The only evil thing a rich person can do is either bury his money in the yard or light their cigars with it taking the cash out of circulation. We all need wealth to survive. Our existence depends on the circulation of wealth. Wealth must first be created and then circulated. If a substantial amount of that circulation is dedicated to more wealth creation the pool of wealth expands and gives more people access to more wealth and there is your real "social justice". As long as a rich person's money is left in circulation everyone can benefit from it…in other words, the rich person is creating social justice. The politician foments division among groups to shield himself from scrutiny. Obama supports the teachers unions but sends his kids to private school: Al Gore flies his pollution spewing jet to global warming events; all overlooked if they are willing to attack conservatives. If he can foster a deep emotional hatred from his supporters against a rival political faction, (the poor against the rich i.e.) the politician's supporters will accept blatant abuse by the politician as long as he appears to be causing harm to the enemy that he manufactured.

If true socialists construct non-governmental voluntary collectives, those entities will evolve purely on the basis of benefit to the members with no consideration of the politician's political ambitions. If the collective model is wildly successful it will dominate based of its own merit. It will not need government coercion to gain membership; its success will provide that. And the collective can achieve its goals without abusing the wealth creator thus allowing for a larger pool of wealth available to benefit the collective. Private collectives are better at redistributing wealth because they do so for the benefit of its members; the politician redistributes wealth solely based on his political needs. Capitalists and socialists can coexist better together than apart. The politician provides very little to the equation and is not worthy of the power he now enjoys. If the capitalist and the socialist can unite against the politician it would create a new era of human advancement.

Wealth's only purpose is to allow individuals to purchase products and services. Voluntary socialism allows the collective to maximize their purchasing power by pooling their wealth and labor, and through the economics of scale getting more goods and services for the individual. Whether a capitalist or member of a collective, an individual can only use wealth by putting it into circulation which is the true route to the redistribution of wealth. Voluntary collectives can assist society by helping a greater number of individuals gain access to the flow of ever increasing wealth streams. The government socialist is a parasite that drains the wealth flow without providing societal benefit while at the same time sickening his wealth creating host.

The attempt by selfish politicians to demonize wealth creators has denied generations of Americans the knowledge to benefit by having more access to the wealth that circulates all around them. But by providing the knowledge of basic economics to government dependents living near poverty, the Live Free Movement can realize real change. And access to increased wealth can be a powerful motivator for the dependent. While I'm sure there are some dependents that prefer doing nothing and collecting a substandard benefit, the vast majority would prefer a hugely improved standard of living the free market offers. They are held back by their lack of knowledge as to how to access the wealth flowing around them. We call it winning the 'hearts and minds' but if we can win the mind the hearts will follow.

Chapter 8

Futurevision

"The wave of the future is not the conquest of the world by a single dogmatic creed but the liberation of the diverse energies of free nations and free men." **John F. Kennedy**

'The vision thing'

Politicians think in terms of 2, 4 or 8 year objectives. And their most important objective is to get elected, the quality of your social needs as a tax payer come in second. In the private sector people are free from the 2, 4, 6 year cycle of Washington. But what we don't seem to appreciate enough is 20, 40 and 60 years out into the future; New born to retirement; 60-70 years. Take a bite out of the welfare state in 20 years. Cripple it in 40 years and be done with it in 60 years. The New Deal was started 75 years ago, you're not going to repeal it over night, and not even in 8 years, and you can't begin to roll it back without a vibrant functioning long term alternative.

That's why the "Vision Thing" (as George H Bush called it) is so important. What will the world look like in 50 or 100 years? Just look back 100 years ago. The plane had just been invented and the auto industry was brand new. There was no New Deal and the financial institutions we see today were in their infancy. It is obvious that there will be equally deep changes in our technology, standard of living and our social and cultural futures in the coming century. Small steps we take today could have a profound impact on the future of the nation or the world for that matter.

Looking at winning an election in the next few years as an end within itself and proposing a platform that is designed to win that one election without weighing its long term impact is not what the Live Free Movement is about. Especially if the long term vision of conservatism is to actually shrink government. Republicans will never be able to out bid Democrats in offering government handouts. If the right accepts that growing government dependency is unavoidable and seeks to attach itself to that gravy train, our future is bleak.

Throughout the early years of the Cold War it was just accepted that Soviet expansion was inevitable. US foreign policy was centered on containment...slowing the growth of expanding communism. It wasn't until Ronald Reagan replaced that vision from containing communism to rolling it back was real progress made, and it didn't take that long for the Soviet Union to fall. The USSR was a flawed system from its inception, it wasn't until Reagan that anyone had the courage and future vision to challenge it and exploit its weaknesses. The American socialist welfare state has many of the same structural flaws that the old Soviet Union had, America just needs men of vision who can exploit those flaws and help it crumble under its own weight.

'What could be?'

Most of the pop culture visions of the future tend to be apocalyptic. We are going to destroy the planet with our pollution or our WMDs so why bother planning for the future since if we survive we'll be rummaging through an inhabitable wasteland? But what if there is another future; one that is a little more boring for sci-fi movie makers but maybe more realistic. If we look at past trends and extend them out, we may be able to make some future predictions as to what today's newborns might find when they reach retirement in 65 years.

We've seen a huge reduction in global poverty over the last 50 years and there is no reason that this trend won't continue and even accelerate. The globalization of capital allows manufacturing to chase cheap labor around the world. But as it enters a poverty stricken nation it begins to create and expand a middle class and eliminate poverty. At some point wage demands begin to rise and cheap labor pools begin to dry up, at that point manufacturing moves on looking for new cheap labor sources. S. Korea is a perfect example. In 1959 S. Korea had a per capita GDP of only $1,110. Today S. Korea's per capita GDP is $25,000. In the 1990s the industrialized world lamented the loss of manufacturing jobs to the cheap labor markets of China but today it is the Chinese who turn a wary eye to Africa as the quest for cheap labor begins to migrate to a new continent. And left behind in China is a swelling middle class that demands consumer products.

At some point this century the global supply of cheap labor will begin to dry up, just as the demand for affordable consumer products will sky rocket. Luckily, just as cheap human labor dries up, technology will be bringing cheap robotic labor on line. By the end of this century the human condition will have evolved to the point where dangerous, menial and laborious work conditions will become a thing of the past.

50 years ago most cancer was lethal. Today, advances in medical science make most cancers treatable and survivable. The talk today is of coming up with a cure for aging, yes aging is being considered more of a disease than a natural part of life. If the advances in medicine over the last 50 years are extended outward we can assume that many of today's diseases will be curable or preventable. And with technological advances in safety reducing accidental deaths it's reasonable that a majority of children born today may well live past their 100th birthday.

Another trend we've seen over the last 50 years is that industrialized countries with a dominate middle class tend to experience population stabilization. As the global middleclass expands and poverty declines, it's quite likely that the global population will stop growing. Technological advances in agriculture and environmental science mean that a stabilized global population could begin to live harmoniously with the environment by the end of the century. The idea is not for man to regress to the agrarian existence of the 18th century but to advance to the Star Trekian existence of the 23rd century where poverty and pollution are eliminated.

If you add up these possible outcomes what you'll see is a world where people routinely live 100+ years. They'll work in a clean safe environment for the first 60 years of their life and enjoy retirement the last 40 years. Working yourself to the bone and then dying won't be the norm for the human condition anymore. More humans will have the free time to contribute to the arts and sciences and expand humanities knowledge pool....or at least really work hard on their golf game. With a stabilized population this means a perpetual system where half of the younger generation is working while the other 50% is retired. With the vast majority of manufacturing and supplying of consumer products provided by robotic labor, the bulk of the world's jobs will be satisfying the leisure time activity demands of retirees. In the future there will be a lot less auto workers and many more travel agents.

Of course Social Security cannot work in this future world no matter how much lip service politicians give to protecting it. S.S. is a 'pay as you go' system. It was set up when most were expected to die before reaching 65 and it was possible for 9 workers to provide for the retirement of one person. In the future it will be impossible for just one worker to supply all the retirement demands of one retiree. Society will change over this period in ways that we cannot predict. A welfare state that refuses to adapt because it places the protection of its bureaucracy over the satisfaction of its citizens is doomed to fail. A private system can adapt. Larger firms that are slow to adapt will lose business to new upstarts that quickly exploit new consumer demands or shifts in societal norms. Successful innovations that work will spread throughout the system while failed attempts at solutions will quickly be discarded. The welfare state can't do that.

The public would soon expect private firms to solve problems not perpetuate them. Today we see private health insurance firms turning towards illness prevention to lower their costs. They realize that customers who eat healthy, don't smoke and exercise make fewer claims so they offer the incentive of lowered premiums to those that enter healthy lifestyle programs. While these firms take their action to improve their profitability, they end up raising the quality of life for their customers as a byproduct which actually gives more value to the money spent on health insurance premiums. This attitude would prevail in the private sector. Private unemployment insurers would have motivation to find creative ways to help their claimants get back to work. If a pill were invented that immediately ended tobacco addiction, health and life insurance companies would hand them out for to all their smoking customers for free and save billions on future claims.

'Corporatism?'

One of the prevailing sci-fi warnings is the danger of corporatism as the politically dominate system over democracy. This could be a very possible threat but at the same time future wealth creation is dependent on a healthy corporate environment. But in a future where the masses are dependent on the health of the global economy they will be naturally drawn to evolving a government that protects individual freedoms and provides adequate policing of the economy. It's actually the welfare state that invites corporate political involvement. Corporations need to become politically active to lessen the impact that class warfare policies have on their bottom line. With a government lacking confiscatory taxing policies and regulations that responsibly balance the needs of industry and the public good, companies will be less inclined to hire a battery of lawyers and lobbyists and can spend their money on more advantageous social causes…like private school vouchers that create a more productive work force for them to draw from. Who knows, maybe firing the five Washington lobbyists might free up the cash to buy the pollution control equipment they need.

When the present government begins to abandon its burdensome nanny-state responsibilities to the private sector it becomes a lean mean policing machine. Luckily we have a constitution that allows us to maximize our individual freedoms and to protect us from the government's policing overreach. We are a nation of laws. It's our responsibility to write good law. At that point a competent police force fairly enforcing competent law is a good thing. With sane regulation and solid effective law enforcement it becomes easier and more advantageous for the individual to acquire a desired standard of living through legal gain than illegal means. But a balance must be struck. Technological advances used to catch the guilty can also be used to oppress the innocent. The constitution was always designed to perform a balancing act between individual freedom which can lead to anarchy and law enforcement which can lead to police state oppression; there is no reason we can't use The Constitution to strike a balance in the future.

There will need to be a cultural change to evolve into this brave new world. For nearly a century now socialists have slandered the capitalist system. Anti-corporate bigotry is rampant around the world. And it is slander when you consider that private free market capitalism provides the vast majority of social justice in the world by providing meaningful employment to the masses while it is government that promotes anti-capitalist bigotry through class warfare electioneering while wielding all its power at the end of a gun. Ideally our government should be elected by individuals who have the sober wisdom, without the propaganda

217

influences of an obsolete leftist movement, to balance their desires for personal freedom with the need of a healthy economy. And if the government lays out a fair level playing field for businesses to thrive in, the corporate world can concentrate more on the bottom line and less on politics. Why lower profits by sending a politician a huge check when everything's going fine and you'd prefer that they just left things the way they were.

The first steps that conservatives can take today without government involvement is to develop a long term education and promotion initiative to dispel anti-capitalist bias. Fight to win in the class warfare battle: Maybe a Capitalist Anti-defamation League. It's imperative that society sees the corporate community for what it really is and not by the misrepresentations of the class warriors. Corporations and small business are our life blood but they can also be powerful oppressors. Sane regulation is required that allows business to prosper while protecting society from their encroachment on our freedom.

Global business concerns have always been and will continue to be politically powerful and influential. But in a society where we recognize the benefits we receive from a healthy economic environment and see the corporate community as a symbiotic partner and less as parasitical host we can limit corporate to government power accumulation by making their cooperative interaction unnecessary.

'A brave new world'

The book "1984" predicted a world where the government knew all and saw all. It called itself "Big Brother" but in reality we've seen the world evolve with the "anti-big brother". It is the average citizen who through the internet can see everything the government is doing. And yes the government tries to monitor as much of the population as possible but at some point that task becomes so monumental that wading through that much information becomes difficult to impossible. All the while the non-governmental masses have the resources to sift through the government's actions sounding the alarm every time they misstep. In the future the transparency of governments will grow with or without their consent. A moral citizenry with the right to vote can eventually bring down the most powerful leaders. The power the ruling elite gain today from exploiting the dependency class will not last. The welfare state is an abomination of the 20th century. It is obsolete, harmful and is destine for collapse.

Even Oppressive regimes in China or Iran will have their actions displayed around the world for all to see. It was Martin Luther King Jr. who said, *"Injustice anywhere is a threat to justice everywhere."* He also said, *"All men are caught in an inescapable network of mutuality."* These prophetic lines will have great meaning in the future. The fact that we can see videos of injustice anywhere in the world on our computers combined with our ability to use the internet to feel a sense of personal relationship with people all over the planet is beginning to pressure oppressive leadership into reform even if that reform isn't totally visible yet. Just as the economy has gone global, so too will basic human rights. At some time in this century oppression will no longer be tolerated.

Today much of the world's activist community is wasted trying to prop up an illegitimate welfare state. Once the fraud of governmental socialism is exposed and put to rest, that activist community will begin to focus on real social justice especially in countries that are ignored today because their socialist façade blinds the politically correct to their true oppressive nature. When individual human rights become the focus of today's leftists, change will come. All warfare today is caused by the attempt at aggressive expansion of totalitarians followed by the defense of human rights. When the world's "Peace Movement" finally decides to topple totalitarianism instead of propping up socialism, warfare can be ended. And along with it comes a global peace dividend that would help finance a huge rise in the global standard of living.

If every single individual on the planet defends basic human rights and every government on the planet was elected and conducted a pacifist foreign policy, the American Military/Industrial Complex would evaporate without the leftist peace movement having to conduct a single protest. The peace activist movement is wasting its time. It can't bring down America's military until it destroys America's enemies. And it could do so. It brought down South Africa's Apartheid government; it could bring down the Iranian regime if it tried. The sad part is that within the leftist activist movement are a large number of individuals who think they are fighting for social justice and human rights but they are being exploited by government elitists and end up only propping up corrupt bureaucracies that merely benefit politicians. When the Live Free movement finally brings down the reign of the socialist politician, left wing activists can finally be set free to combat the globe's real injustice; totalitarianism.

———————————————

'Live Free: 200 years in the future'

In this book we've been examining the Live Free Movement's effect 65 years into the future but maybe we should look even further out ahead. In 65 years Live Free has changed the face of American culture. Poverty has been almost eliminated and the small amount that remains is completely manageable. Because of the absence of the trillions of dollars once spent on the welfare state, the standard of living for every American has risen to unimaginable heights, that wealth instead has been invested into technology. Healthcare, the environment, safety, transportation, communication and agriculture have all advanced exponentially, pointing to a future of perpetual sustainability.

And because the Live Free Movement is non-governmental and so effective it has been spreading around the world. It has toppled many oppressive regimes along with many of the planets socialist governments. Global poverty is beginning to disappear and warfare is rare. The global population has leveled off and economists around the world are beginning to debate the effects of the end of economic growth and its replacement; economic maintenance. The food and water supply for the world's population is sustainable and the end of hunger is an attainable goal for humanity.

As the year 2100 approaches our educational system is giving all children a chance to learn at a level we could only imagine today. Political correctness has been replaced with truth. Children grow up understanding that they as individuals provide value to society not as a member of a political party or victimized group. In history class they learn of governmental socialism as a failed thing of the past like feudalism, Nazism or fascism. The US Constitution is alive and well and actually respected. Our present day turmoil is studied as a lesson on the fragility of our freedom and the responsibility of individuals to defend it for future generations.

Since children are no longer exploited by being held up as 'victims', seen only by their value to the advancement of the ruling elite's power base, they are expected universally to contribute to the betterment of society and they do rise to those expectations. Most importantly children are no longer taught anti-capitalism. They are graduating with a healthy understanding of the working environment they will be entering. Children no longer see limitations imposed on them by society, like the notion that they are held back by their race or gender. Instead they realize early that their only limitations are self imposed.

By the end of the 22nd century the earth's human population will
have stabilized for nearly 100 years. Energy technology is clean
efficient and cheap. Agriculture is stabilized, sustainable and
environmentally friendly. Nearly all of the planet's citizens are
living as independent individuals with a clear understanding of
the tenets of freedom. In a world of responsible individuals the
need or desire of a ruling class has been eliminated. And with all
the planets resources sustainable, renewable, recycled and
attainable, the need for resource wars are gone. Free individuals
have become the world's overwhelming power base and the
governments they tolerate work exclusively on the behalf of the
free individual.

'Live Free and save the planet'

We hear so much talk about saving the planet but that can only be
achieved by the elimination of poverty. Increases in living
standards lead to population stabilization and the increased
application of pollution controls and technologies. Put a
population of poor people in a region that gets cold and if they
have no other means they will cut down every tree to the horizon
for heat. They will kill every animal for food without regard to

their endangered species status. Without treatment plants they will defecate and urinate directly into the nearest waterway. It's not that they don't care; it's just that poor people don't have the means to save the planet. Sorry but fixing the environment costs money and unfortunately we are spending the majority of our national treasure on a needless welfare state. If the recipients were out creating wealth instead of finding creative ways to keep their governmental sustenance income flowing, we'd have a much greater ability to work on the environment. Poor people's cars are older and have worse gas mileage; their homes are less likely to be insulated. Small businesses struggling in high tax cities are less likely to upgrade to more efficient machinery.

In the future when socialism is dying our planet will become cleaner. With more money in their pockets average folks will be able to afford green products. More Americans will be driving newer and cleaner cars. They will be buying new windows reducing their heating costs. Businesses will be taking the money they once sent to the government and spending it on new equipment thus reducing their per unit energy costs. Municipalities will be able to invest in improved water treatment plants. States not burdened with unpaid mandates from Washington will be better able to devote more revenue towards meaningful cleanup projects. Go to any liberal run big city and you'll see two things; poverty and filth, the two go hand in hand.

Any progressive socialist can point out that there is pollution but it takes a wealth creator to clean it up.

'One, two, three, four: Live Free and end the war'

If we examine our history over the last century we find some interesting comparisons. Most if not all the warfare can be defined as a totalitarian trying to expand his power or territory engaged by free men trying to stop him. Whether fascism, communism or radical Islam, it all boils down to a group of elitists who deny individual rights and seek to expand their power. Even the Israeli-Palestinian conflict can be reduced to this same formula. The Israelis and Palestinians would have reached a negotiated settlement 60 years ago but dictators in Iran, Syria and Saudi Arabia perpetuate the war by funding their mercenary forces Hamas and Hezbollah. It's interesting to note that when Iraq's dictatorship died, so did Iraq's support of the Israel-Palestine war.

Today we see one of the most oppressive regimes in the world in Iran. Its citizens cry out for support to achieve their most basic human rights but are completely ignored by the people in our own country who accept the mantle of 'the protectors of human rights'. America's activist community is so wrapped up in protecting the socialist power structure and the position of elitist leftist politicians that they are blind to real human suffering around the world. TV images of Iranian's protesting for their freedom then brutally being put down generates no response from America's leftists, but even a rumor of a potential tax cut will fill the streets with an angry mob demanding their pet government program be not just spared but expanded. This is because "social justice" has been redefined from protecting basic human rights to protecting the welfare state. If these Iranians were demanding a redistribution of wealth from America's so called "rich" instead of their own personal freedom you can bet they'd have the left's undivided attention.

But in the future when the power of the socialist politician begins to crumble, the activists will begin to search for a new cause, after all, protesting is what they do. As poverty, hunger and hopelessness begin to fade they will by default revert to what should be their real cause; basic individual freedom. The world's activist leftists marching in the streets demanding Iranian regime change would inspire average Iranians and force Western governments to enact sanctions with teeth and it would topple the Iranian regime. The Mullahs would have no choice but to flee the country or have their citizens offer up a ride on a Mussolini swing set. The day will come when political activists see toppling totalitarian regimes as sport.

What history has taught us is that democratic nations of free people tend not to go to war with each other. In a world where every single human has protected voting rights, war is very unlikely. In a world of rising standards of living and decreasing populations, warfare for territorial expansion becomes unimportant. In a world of rapid technological advancement in food and energy production, environmental protection and industrial raw material management, resource wars become unnecessary.

'Can we really predict the future?'

With precision? No. But if we plant an acorn and nurture it, we can be reasonably assured that in the future we will have a giant oak tree. In the same way, if we envision what it is we want to accomplish decades in the future we can plant those seeds today.

While we don't know exactly what our visions will evolve into, with a clear eye on our final objectives we can prune our society to achieve any goal we desire.

When FDR planted the seeds of the giant socialist state he had an idea that it would grow into a significant political power source for decades to come, he just didn't know what form it would take and how intrusive it would become. While some people warned at the time of the looming danger, very few could have imagined the enormity that today's federal government would grow into. But we have the advantage of seeing socialism evolve for a century. We know where its weaknesses and its short comings are. We know how the socialists will react to challenge and we even know what language and tactics they will use to fight back. Because we are working long term we can design our tactics and initiatives to slowly erode socialism until it fades away.

America is a nation of dreamers. We dream up new ideas everyday and we set out to make them real. In the 60s there was a man who had a dream. At the time his dream might have seemed impossible to achieve but his dream was right and moral. It's been over 50 years but that dream has changed our culture and the world. Dreams that are worthwhile can live for a long time and bring real change. The dream of a Live Free society can survive the test of time because it is right and moral. If we are patient but determined in 50 years we will see that our efforts are bearing fruit.

Chapter 9

Tax Reform

"Governments last as long as the under taxed can defend themselves against the overtaxed."

Bernard Berenson

'Enhancing Privatization'

Unfortunately America's tax codes are something that has to be addressed from within the government. But by converting citizens from government dependents to rugged individualists you increase political pressure to accommodate that growing segment of voters. And for the vast majority of them, the burden of an inefficient welfare state will affect their voting habits. As the number of people not dependent on the state grows so will the demand for tax relief.

Taxes have two functions to the politician. First is to collect revenue to run the country, but to the socialist politician it is a means to control behavior. Punitive taxes placed on tobacco are less about raising money than they are about reducing smoking. Unfortunately this also applies to income taxes; they discourage acquiring income. People are actually discouraged from moving to a higher income bracket for fear of taxation. The government also provides tax breaks for donations the state deems worthy instead of donating to organizations the individual prefers. As the level of taxation becomes excessive, the more subservient the average citizen becomes to the politician in an effort to avoid paying those taxes. In the same way, tax breaks are doled out by the politician to bribe corporations and certain industries into subservience.

Taxes are a necessary evil but their impact and acceptance by society reflects the population's perception of how the money is spent and collected. If the average citizen perceives his government as beneficial and his tax rate as fair, he is much more likely to be compliant and content with paying them. Politicians constantly talk about taxes as "paying your fair share" but that is another Orwellian double speak term. Today's tax code is designed to be radically unfair because it punishes wealth creation and rewards government dependency.

It's sometimes difficult to see the relationship between our tax codes and the breakdown of the nation's moral fiber but it exists. We think of taxes mostly in terms of our income taxes. But we also pay property taxes. Even if we rent the landlord's property taxes are worked into our rent along with his income tax obligation. We pay gas taxes and we pay sales taxes. We buy products whose price includes the taxes the manufacturers have paid. In the end we pay nearly 50% of our incomes in taxes most of which are hidden from us. We get excited when a politician promises to tax the evil rich guy but we never consider that the rich guy simply passes those tax burdens down to us in the price of the products we buy.

A family's bread winner might be able to provide for the living expenses of the family but is usually unable to cover the cost of the 50% tax obligation. That means that the other parent must surrender their duty of child rearing to enter the work force for the sole purpose of paying the government. This leaves children abandoned to the clutches of the socialist school system to provide not only basic knowledge but moral standards. And because of its monopoly America's government run school system ends up with a majority of the nation's children. It's not surprising that the government school system teaches blind allegiance to an expanding government bureaucracy and the worship of the uber-powerful politician as its main curriculum. It will be difficult to change the culture while the government is "dumbing down" future generations.

If we accept the notion that politicians are unworthy of the responsibility of engineering our society and have no business dictating America's culture because of their own corruption, we need to design our future tax codes more on their ability to raise revenue and less on their behavioral modification aspects. Today all discussion on tax code changes are considered in terms of increasing revenue or at least "revenue neutrality", but our troubles with enormous deficit spending has nothing to do with taxes, it's caused by runaway spending. Trying to imagine the tax codes of the Live Free future in the shadow of today's oppressive government could be counterproductive.

I think it would be advantageous to envision the Live Free world 65 years in the future and then design a tax code that applies. Then we can work our way back and design a system that heads in that direction. In the 2075 Live Free America the free economy has grown to an unbelievable size while our limited government is a mere fraction of what it is today. The priorities of this future government will be more in line with the original intent of the Constitution. Enormous entitlement spending will be gone. The success of the Live Free movement will have spread around the world spreading peace and prosperity and drastically reducing our need for military spending. While our need to police the free market will be an important function of government, the fairness of the sane regulation we impose will encourage legal commerce and discourage fraud so that the policing will be much more effective towards a much smaller problem.

In 2075 very few people will need a government subsidy and most will be taxpayers. But due to the very small size of our limited government in comparison to GDP, the tax obligation of each individual is miniscule. Paying your "fair share" is comfortably attainable by every citizen not just an obligation of the rich. Income taxes are intrusive. They force hundreds of millions of free Americans to reveal intimate aspects of their daily lives to unsympathetic government IRS agents. The abolition of income taxes will lead to a huge increase in personal privacy and drastically contribute to the culture's separation of the citizen from the government. Today the government socialists use the income and wealth based taxes as a cattle prod to force the citizenry into conforming to demands of the welfare state. For example; the inheritance tax makes it more likely that your heirs will not have the benefit of your wealth so they would be more likely to become future government dependents. Right now people weigh the tax implications of what they put in their IRAs and the government puts limits on what a person can invest with tax exempt status. Without income taxes, if a person wishes to live a frugal life style and spend less and save more, over their life time they would pay fewer taxes. They should not be punished for this. They are lessening potential obligations the government might have towards them in the future and they are allowing their wealth to be used as capital to create jobs in the economy thus lessening the demand for government hand outs. They may be paying fewer taxes but they are doing their fair share for society. Joe Biden needs to learn that being a capital investor is just as patriotic as being a tax payer.

If we eliminate the income tax we should examine its replacement. Some sort of consumption tax might be advantageous to our society but we must carefully consider their overall affect on the economy and society. Consumption taxes come in a variety of forms. There is a direct retail sales tax, a Value Added Tax (VAT) or it's possible to tax raw commodities before they are manufactured. Sales taxes are a fair tax in the sense that everyone pays the same rate without consideration to their financial standing. It also allows for foreign tourists to contribute to our tax base when they purchase products within our borders. The advantage of a sales tax over a VAT or commodity tax is that it allows American businesses to manufacture products without increasing their cost by putting the taxes into the price. This allows American products to be exported at a lower cost and increases American competiveness. The down side of a sales tax is they lose the progressive nature of taxes that are common in today's tax code. But that can be addressed but subsidizing the taxes of the poor at the beginning. It's important to remember that our objective is to wipe out poverty. A subsidy would be expected to be phased out as more and more people climb out of poverty and become ineligible for the subsidy.

A commodity tax could be beneficial but only in the respect that it addresses national problems caused by the extraction or use of the commodity. For example: today's Cap and Trade legislation could be a good model if the politician could be trusted to use it to actually fight pollution as opposed to expanding coercive socialism. In the future where the power lust of the politician has been neutered we may be able to examine cap and trade formulas on their merit alone. But simply directly taxing a commodity based on its environmental impact might be the wisest course. A big enough tax on mercury will encourage its replacement throughout manufacturing. Direct taxation on smokestack output will limit all the chemicals released not just CO_2. Direct taxes on fossil fuels will encourage alternatives. In a future where the nation's tax burden has been drastically reduced it might be difficult to tax a commodity to the point where it affects its overall usage, but this could be a good thing. Say you have a national sales tax rate of .04% but you want to tax crude oil to encourage alternate fuels. You might raise enough revenue from the commodity tax to allow the sales tax rate to drop to .03%. The drop in the sales tax rate will stimulate economic growth that offsets the impact of the commodity tax. The problem lies in the fact that using the tax code to foster environmental change is counterproductive if not done on a global level. If the effort only transfers the pollution to another country then it is a failure. If American businesses are forced through taxation to remove mercury from their products but China still does, the American businesses that could innovate new non-mercury products might be driven out of business leaving only the Chinese products available to all. National commodity taxes in a global economy must be carefully crafted and global treaties need to be an important component. Of course there is the option of applying a commodity tax at the retail end of a product; taxing a harmful commodity based on its content within a product. This way both the Chinese and American product containing mercury will be more expensive than the one without. This would drive the market on a global basis to reduce the use of the harmful commodity as a natural drive for competitiveness. Unfortunately today the global socialists have hijacked the environmental movement to advance the power of the politician and have hampered the ability of real environmentalists to actually clean up the planet.

In today's big government environment it's difficult to think of changes in the way we tax ourselves. The politicians who write our tax laws have a vested interest in perverting our tax codes to benefit themselves with little consideration of the economic impact of their decisions. But we must be able to see beyond the era of the predatory politician. If we were to convert from an income tax to a national sales tax today we may have to impose a rate 0f 10%, 12% or even 15% to maintain the revenue neutrality the politician today would surely require. But a tax rate like that would discourage consumption and encourage savings. The added income provided by the repeal of the income tax would offset the increase of taxes at the retail level. If you move to some sort of consumption tax and abolish income taxes you eliminate the incentive to spend your income on investments the government deems as worthy of tax exempt status. You would be able to invest in an IRA with no consideration to its tax ramifications what so ever. Instead of trying to hide your money from the government, you can freely invest in the products that maximize the return for your future social needs.

———————————

'Power in Numbers'

Again the need for conservative unity comes into play. Deciding on one tax plan and promoting it in unison is vital. Today the right is split between the fair tax plan, the flat tax plan and much debate is put into the "revenue neutrality" of any change. The argument goes that "any change has to maintain this big bloated welfare state we have right now." As free Americans we need to look ahead for the most beneficial taxation method for when the welfare state is dismantled and begin the first steps to head in that direction. We need to have a debate as to the proper course of action but once that debate is settled we need to quickly jump on the band wagon and begin to force the politician to bend to our will. The politician will first attempt to ignore us then he will try to demonize us but if we stay firm and resolute and base his condition of re-election on the reform of the tax code he will eventually capitulate. At this point in time a switch of our tax structure is unlikely. Our tax system is less about obtaining revenue and more about control. Income taxes are about creating a huge pool of dependents that pay no taxes but claim sustenance benefits who will vote for the socialist politician. While it's been proven over and over again that lower tax rates actually increase revenue by increasing economic growth and the number of tax payers, socialist politicians routinely oppose them because economic growth moves people away from their place as government dependents. People who don't collect a government benefit are less likely to vote for a socialist. In our present system the health of the economy always takes a back seat to the maintenance of the welfare state. But the Live Free Movement will slowly erode the welfare state and with it the balance of political power. The time will come sooner than later where changing the tax code will be politically possible and we should be prepared to maximize the opportunity.

In the mean time the push for tax reform can become a weapon we use to constantly attack and humiliate the politician. Today's tax system has a huge block of people who don't pay taxes. They don't care how high taxes are but they do want more benefits. This system is designed solely by the socialist politician for the pure benefit of the socialist politician. It's designed by a majority to confiscate the wealth of a minority. The objective truth is that it is those people in America who don't pay taxes but use government resources paid for by someone else's hard work who are the real ones who are not paying "their fair share". One of the most important truths free people need to make is to be able to point out that fact with conviction and not be intimidated by the left's attacks. Real "compassion" comes by motivating individuals to push themselves into a life of self reliance; if tough love does it than it is a compassionate act. The message must be concise and repeated over and over again. The idea that the income tax is corrupt needs to become simply common knowledge. It must be repeated that those who don't pay taxes need to begin pulling their weight. If nothing else just get the hell out of the way and let the rest of us fight for reform.

The Live Free Movement is designed so that our numbers gradually grow and because we are educated, active and united our efforts to challenge the system can be effective. When the political elite tried to push through an amnesty bill that undermined the rule of law in America the people spontaneously arose and scared the hell out of the ruling class and they buckled. The irresponsible spending and the national healthcare push in 2009 caused an uprising at town hall meetings that made Nancy Pelosi cry from sheer fear for her personal safety. These examples reveal the undercurrent that represents the power of the Live Free Movement. Without organization, unity and direction the power of this movement was still able to strike fear in the hearts of the socialist politician. Imagine the power the movement will brandish when it discovers its identity and is able to recruit and expand its numbers exponentially.

Chapter 10

Nationalizing the Legal Profession

"It is the lawyers who run our civilization for us -- our governments, our business, our private lives. Most legislators are lawyers; they make our laws. Most presidents, governors, commissioners, along with their advisers and brain-trusters are lawyers; they administer our laws. All the judges are lawyers; they interpret and enforce our laws. There is no separation of powers where the lawyers are concerned. There is only a concentration of all government power -- in the lawyers. "- **FRED RODELL**

'Let's have some fun'

This is just a debating tool I use to really throw the socialists off their message, so don't take this too seriously. OK, so here we go: **Nationalize the legal profession.**

It works like this; all lawyers become government employees with a union, very similar to postal workers. (I had a friend suggest we make them wear a little uniform with shorts.) They earn between $35,000 to $65,000 a year, with their salaries determined by seniority not performance. When someone goes to court they are assigned the next lawyer on the list by the government. It doesn't matter how rich or poor you are you get the exact same level of representation. Do away with lawyers making a percentage on multimillion dollar awards, win or lose the lawyer will still earn his $65,000 union negotiated salary. Do away with the obscene windfall profits and the greed within the legal profession.

OK, so I'm not really serious here but this is a great argument. Whenever I'm in a group of left leaning folk who are making a passionate argument on the virtues of nationalized health care, energy, the auto industry or some other industry, I bring up this discussion claiming that the legal profession should lead the way and prove to the others the superior elegance of socialism. There is nothing more fun than being in a room of leftists watching them argue why socialism sucks, while of course under cutting all their arguments on the brilliance of nationalizing this or that.

While my national legal care program isn't serious I think it can be a useful tool on the national level. Let's face it, the motto in Washington DC today is: *"Government of the lawyers, by the lawyers, for the lawyers, shall not perish from the Earth."* Data compiled by Robert Schmults of the Heritage Foundation, a Washington-based think tank, and Investor's Business Daily, indicates that about 40% of the 535 members of Congress are attorneys. This includes over half of US senators. And let's remember that Washington's politicians are not there selflessly advocating for the betterment of humanity, they get elected to advance their own greedy ambitions for power and socialized legal care strikes them right between their greedy little eyes. And you can bet that Washington's ruling elite will throw socialism under the bus in a heartbeat when it threats their own little cocoon.

The typical argument I get from the devoted leftist is "If you get in legal trouble don't you want the best representation money can buy???" To which my stock reply is "Yea, and when I get sick I want the best medical representation I can buy!"

But while this mind game is a hoot to play when debating your left wing friends out in public, it does have some merit to consider. The vast majority of America's ruling class socialists are Ivy League educated lawyers but why pay a Harvard tuition just to get a $65,000 a year union job? Let neighborhood community colleges graduate the lawyers. That would be an eye opener for Harvard though wouldn't it. They'd have to totally change their curriculum. Maybe they could switch to graduating socialist economists. That would be better for us. They wouldn't be running around the country suing everything that moves and better yet very few would be going into government to rob us blind. Basically they'd be sitting around writing books about socialism that no one reads except each other, and America will be better for it.

America wins by having less socialist sponsored tax legislation (not to mention having our legislation written in English and not legalese), Less law suits which mean less expensive products throughout the country and much less pain in the ass regulations for average Americans to have to break in their day to day lives.

The United States has about 50% of the world's lawyers. An advantage of the $65,000 union salary caps is that a huge number of Americans will skip the legal profession altogether and enter more lucrative professions like medicine, or science…or sanitation engineering.

So maybe we should start a national movement. "Layers First!" You want to nationalize healthcare?? "Lawyers First!" You want to nationalize the Banks?? "Lawyers First!" Get Washington so caught up in defending the legal profession from nationalization that they don't have time to nationalize anything else.

So how do we get this ball rolling? Well first, if this were a bill introduced to Congress it would get buried so fast in committee it would make your head spin. But maybe a state ballot initiative? After all we're looking more for shock value than real legislation. Just imagine collecting signatures to put the "Screw the Lawyers" initiative on the ballot. Every prominent lawyer around the country would flock to that state prepared to do battle… and along with them TV crews from around the nation. Look at all the money you could make selling "Screw the Lawyers" T-shirts.

Once the average American sees how fun it is to drive a bunch of lawyers completely insane, everybody will want to start a fight in their state. Get the lawyers so involved in defending their profession that they don't have time to run around the country suing everyone else. And with lawyers being desperate not to end up as union schmucks, they might just be willing to consider some common sense tort reform in exchange for their own butts.

On the other hand the lawyers will fight back with expert precision. They will brilliantly use the American legal system to undermine socialized legal aid. And in the process they will set a wealth of precedence and case law that will be used against all forms of government socialism.

The reality is that in the Live Free world of the future personal responsibility will be a cornerstone and must be reflected in our legal system. It's imperative for free people who live together in harmony to have a fair objective tort system to resolve disputes peaceably. Citizens must be compensated for their legitimate loses but at the same time defendants must be protected against predatory law suits that are initiated for profit with no regard for justice. The incestuous relationship between lawyers and politicians who rig the system for their own personal gain cannot be battled from within that system. Reducing their overall relevance and access to money from the outside is important. The "Screw the Lawyer" movement might shake things up.

Another great tactic would be to use state ballot initiative to regulate the legal profession like crazy; exponentially more red tape to become a lawyer and even more to stay one. We could write some doozies too. Like: *You need to practice law for 2 years before you can take the bar exam but you can't practice law unless you pass the exam.* Or how about state level windfall profit taxes, maybe 95% on the lawyer's share of winning cases. You know, kind of like the taxes they want to impose on Wall Street employees.

With each new regulation (whose violation is considered a disbarrable felony) that you throw at the ability of a person to become or remain in the legal profession you get a percentage who say the "hell with it" and drop out. (Kind of like doctors do when you nationalize medicine) And the more radical and ridiculous the proposals to "screw the lawyers" become the more reasonable common sense tort reform proposals begin to look.

In the 2000 page Obamacare nationalized healthcare bill our ruling lawyers in the White House or the legislature couldn't even propose a paragraph of tort reform even though every American knows that reform will lower healthcare costs. Politician lawyers in Washington have their campaign coffers exploding with money stolen from frivolous law suits; they have no intention of touching that cash cow. But if a wind fall profits tax at the state level begins to sweep the nation, the boys in Washington might just consider negotiating. "Knock that tax down to 85% and we'll give you awards caps. 75% and we'll consider 'loser pays'.

Personally I think it is sad that the average American has to get radical simply to put some 'justice' back into our justice system but I guess that's what we get for letting our politicians erode our liberty over the last century. It was Shakespeare who said, "Let's kill all the lawyers". I think scaring the hell out of them would be just as effective.

Conclusion

In writing this book I was always searching for new and creative ways to combat the growing oppression of our government and without exception every idea I had always fit perfectly with the original intent of our United States Constitution. While I've always had a deep respect for the document, I am still amazed at how well our Founding Fathers understood the dangers of runaway government and how carefully they crafted the Constitution to provide for us the means to battle back. But our founders also knew and expressly warned us that with our freedom we also possessed the freedom to surrender our liberty and over the last 200 years that's exactly what we did. It was Benjamin Franklin who said, *"Those who would give up essential liberty to purchase a little temporary safety deserve neither liberty nor safety."* The message from our founders was clear: We leave you this brilliant document for future generations to live with liberty and prosperity but each and every citizen has an obligation to protect the Constitution from the encroachment of the tyrant…and we failed. Luckily for America it seems that our original Constitution allows us to regain the freedom that we neglectfully capitulated. The Declaration of Independence reminds us that as human beings we have "inalienable rights" of freedom and liberty. We simply have to stand as one and proclaim them.

Throughout the history of mankind rulers have always gained power by suppressing the rights of their subjects, and at some point the ruler always gains enough power to treat his subjects with contempt and as usual we are seeing that take place in America today. The US Constitution is the first document every created by man that forces the leaders of a government to be subservient to its average citizens. But our ruling class has decided that it can simply add invisible, imagined clauses into our Constitution or just ignore amendments that hinder their quest for power. But that original Constitution still exists. Those imaginary clauses have not been written in and no amendments have been blotted out and that document is ours not theirs. At any time we can stand up and reclaim it. If a century from now we are successful at rolling back the tyrants, our Constitution will still guide us well. It will be just as fresh, just as new as the day it was written. And if it does "evolve" it will do so by our request through the proper amendment procedure.

The politician has eroded our liberty little by little over a long period of time. We don't need a bloody revolution, we can simple turn the tables and erode the politician's power little by little over a long period of time. Whole sale change right now today is a lost cause. The attempt will fail because too many people would suffer in the process. The 75 year old lady who has no income except Social Security will sell her granddaughter into bankruptcy to keep her check coming because starvation is her only other option. And we don't want her to starve because she just might be our mother. But we damn well want to make sure that when her granddaughter is 75 that she doesn't have only a pitiful government check standing between her and death.

We can't change America over night but we can change America. Many of our fellow citizens who were completely apathetic just a few short years ago are today stunned by the sheer magnitude of the corruption and waste that the Washington politician doesn't even bother to hide anymore. The level of arrogance and contempt displayed by our leaders only shows that they feel their power has grown to the point where they no longer have to fear the wrath of the American voter. They feel once healthcare is under government control, the American people will have no choice but to bow down to their masters, so why bother pretending to be concerned about average people's interests. But the American people are waking up; slowly stirring and the Washington politician has no clue as to the giant they have roused. The problem is that it's hard to see a solution. Replacing Republicans with Democrats or vice-versa doesn't work so many people feel helplessly alone. But the answer is simple: Self reliance and personal responsibility. That concept can unite all Americans and give them unity and purpose. And the American people with unity and purpose are a power force the Washington politician cannot fathom. It's not about Republican vs. Democrat, it's about citizen vs. politician and the politician will tremble with fear when he sees our mighty silhouette breaching the horizon.

Many of us in our 30s, 40s and beyond will die as government dependents. That's sad but it's a self inflicted wound. Which would be OK if it was just us, but we didn't stop with destroying our own lives, we went ahead and spent our children's and grandchildren's futures for our own selfish comfort. We were too lazy to fix our nation's social problems so we dumped it into the laps of our government who took the opportunity to rob us blind without fixing a damn thing. We were too busy watching the ball game to be bothered with protecting our nation from the tyrants running Washington today. We've screwed our kids and we've screwed them bad. A huge part of personal responsibility is for us to take the responsibility for the mess we've created. No longer can we blame the other side or the other Party or the other race or the other income bracket. I did this, you did this. Confess then repent. We can make amends. While we may not be able to save ourselves we can save our children. We can build a nation where they can live free. We can shield them from the tyrants. We can teach them to shun the government. "Mama, don't let your kids grow up to be dependents." We owe it to them.

It's a two front war. While we educate our kids and provide them with opportunity we must also run interference from the politician that seeks to enslave them. Our kids need things in their lives to survive and thrive. They need food and shelter and many material things. We need to teach them how to work and build them an economy that they can flourish in and protect that economy from the predation of the socialist politician.

They need education. We must destroy the socialist training centers and replace them with institutions of knowledge not propaganda. We must teach them about the Constitution; about freedom and liberty, and how to protect that freedom and not take it for granted like we did. We must teach them about how to live free, why to live free and about the importance of passing down that knowledge to their children to ensure the rise of the tyrant never occurs again.

They need healthcare. We need to leave them a healthcare system that harnesses the innovation and efficiency of the free market; a system that prevents and cures disease not just a system that houses sick people. A system that provides them the most modern up to date care the instant they need it. They'll need a retirement income. We need to help them save from the day they are born. With innovations in medicine they will be retired for nearly half their lives, we must help them prepare. As children and young adults they will not understand the needs of their retirement. We should prepare them to retire without allowing the government to exploit them.

We can help the next generation with these things and we should not only because it is the right thing to do and is good for the future of the nation but because we owe it to them. We already spent their futures on our selfishness. We have an obligation to repay that debt. The socialist politician will do everything he can to entice, coddle, threaten, bribe or outright force our children into the dependency trap. The new SHIPs program is a perfect example of the government targeting our children for a life of dependency. Our job is to interfere with every effort the politician makes; to throw Washington into gridlock. To use every means we can to stop every initiative they can dream up. No matter how compassionate or wonderful a program sounds, if it involves writing a government check to someone then it is to be attacked and destroyed. Band together and take every action the government engages in and challenge it in court; overwhelm the system until it grinds to a halt.

The Live Free Movement is evolutionary. While it will have some noticeable successes and some heart breaking setbacks, in the best case we will wake up one day and realize we are a little freer then we were last year. The growth of the national debt will slow and then gradually diminish. The number of government dependents will progressively shrink and the number of taxpayers will slowly rise. A workers tax obligation will lessen and his IRA will enlarge. Each generation will leave a little more to their grandkids. Each generation will return to being better off than the one before. While we will surely have some heroes who make tremendous contributions to the cause, our real success will be average people making little changes in their day to day lives each adding up to a tidal wave of change.

The Live Free Movement is about changing the culture not winning elections. Its most important element is a simple change in attitude, making self reliance and personal responsibility fashionable again. It's about realizing that the most important contribution you can make to society is to provide for yourself and your family. Yes, giving to your community is a desirable trait but if you first can't provide for yourself and must survive on someone else's hard work you are a net liability not an asset to your community. "How did you help your community today?" "Well, I purchased my own healthcare insurance." Global socialists in their effort to distort the language have tried to demonize the terms "self reliance" and "personal responsibility". The call those words "uncompassionate", "mean spirited", "racist", "judgmental" but with every dollar a person collects from the government it denies a dollar that another human can use to survive. That is a true lack of compassion. A change in attitude is important. Those of us in the Live Free Movement who are unable to escape from dependency can lead the way in changing the attitude about the government benefits we receive. They are not entitlements we are owed, they are gifts of charity that we receive because we failed to be self reliant. While you may want to argue that you paid into the system so you are "entitled", remember you paid into a corrupt Ponzi scheme and are receiving benefits that are bankrupting the nation and are borrowed from future generations. If you can help the nation become humble and honest about their benefits, people naturally prefer to be givers instead of takers and will strive to become a self reliant giver. Most people want to be good citizens, they want to be admired and respected by their family, friends, neighbors and community. By defining being separated from the government as a component of respectability, people will want to find ways to achieve that status.

The natural condition of man is a paradox. We are strongly individual but yet we function best as a member of a collective. A human alone is capable of tremendous accomplishments but when we band together with others in our community it allows the individual to specialize and share their abundance with the entire village. Our ultimate happiness is derived by finding harmony between our individuality and our connection to community. The environment we live in is constantly changing and the survival of any organism is determined by a quick adaption to its changing environment. The natural means that humans use to balance their individual and collective impulses with their changing environment is the free market. The free market is to humans what the hive is to bees. The free market works because it is not pre-planned but reacts to environmental change through millions of actions taken by its individual members. Government by contrast is slow to adjust and is completely unable to keep up with the ever changing environment. While regulation of the free market is necessary, over regulation becomes a pollutant that poisons the environment. If you examine how politicians are elected you find that they are woefully unworthy and unqualified to manage the environment humans exist in. It's ironic that environmentalists are adamant about protecting the natural habitat that all non-human organisms exist in but they advocate the pollution and corruption of man's natural habitat; the free market.

But man's freedom also has a dark side. Without any restraint, individuals can exploit abuse and destroy other individuals. Collectivism allows individuals to unite in common defense but it also allows them to unite in common aggression. This dark side of humanity is what leads to the necessity of government. Government's fundamental role is to protect the individual from abuse from other individuals or groups. But government's only means of exercising its power is through the coercive use of force. Its true mission is to use that force as a neutralizing counter force against the aggression of other abusers. But when government expands its mandate beyond its primary role into areas like social engineering, it itself becomes the abusive aggressor. While society needs government to protect it from humanity's dark side it must always be wary because government itself is just as dangerous as the forces it's meant to protect us from.

Freedom is wonderful. Freedom is what we all strive for and desire. But freedom without responsibility is chaos. In our society today irresponsibility is glorified. Our kids are raised in a pop culture that promotes the 'gangsta' life style above respectable citizenship. We've surrendered not so much our freedom but our responsibility to government but since freedom and responsibility go hand in hand we've surrendered our freedom as a byproduct of capitulating our responsibility. Even though we expect it to, government is unqualified to mandate our moral standards and when it attempts to do so it distorts the delicate balance between our freedom and our responsibility.

For example: The government forces both parents to work so one of them can pay the enormous tax obligation the government imposes on the family. The parents separated from their children then dump the responsibility but not the authority of discipline in the laps of the school system. When the school system does attempt discipline, the parent sues. In order to protect itself the school system adopts zero tolerance policies that end up with 6 year olds being arrested for having plastic knives in their lunch bags. The school system blames the break down in society's moral standards as a failure of the parent. But it is the fact that 50% of the family's income is confiscated in taxes that is to blame. The government is forcing American parents to abandon their responsibility to morally educate their children.

A huge aspect of the Live Free Movement is to re-establish a moral code in America. The politician uses morality to divide Americans. They pit Christians against the gay community hoping both will be politically weaker and unable to challenge the politician but true morality transcends religion or sexual preference. The problem with the battles we face today in regards to moral issues is that groups want to legislate every aspect of their particular moral conventions which means those opposed to those conventions feel they must politically do battle so as not to be considered criminals if they choose to live differently. If the threat of legislation were removed it would be easier for all parties to adopt a 'live and let live attitude'. The goal of the Live Free Movement should be to advance moral standards that apply to all people; ideals of mutual respect, common courtesy, personal responsibility, individual rights, neighborliness, hard work. And most importantly these things don't need to be legislated. To legislate your personal moral code means you need your politician; to just live your personal moral code means the politician can be cut out of the loop.

Our goal is simple right? We want to shrink the size of government. You hear many Republican politicians use those exact words but what does that actually encompass? According to the U.S. Census Bureau, in 2008 the government employed 2.5 million civilian workers. 75 million Baby Boomers will begin to collect Social Security in the next two decades and hundreds of millions of Americans collect some sort of benefit from the government. One thing you can count on for sure is that if you try to take away a penny from any one of them the news media will yank them in front of the cameras and sensationalize a huge sob story about how their kids won't have a Christmas or their grandma will have to choose between cat food and her heart medicine. And for sure the politician who proposed the cut will be shown as a disciple of Satan who practices human sacrifice for fun and kicks puppies on his way to the Capitol. No, you simply cannot elect a politician who will cut government spending.

The reality is that you have only two choices that will shrink government. One is to do nothing and simply let the welfare state grow until the American economy crumbles and then try to pick up the pieces. Of course, whether you'll still have the Constitution or you'll be under the thumb of a dictator is a gamble you'll have to endure.

The second option is to roll up your sleeves, join the Live Free Movement and rescue one government dependent at a time until there are none left. The main stream media is not going to be able to parade out newly freed people who are better off then when they were dependents so you probably won't hear much about the success of our movement from them but you will be able to access the truth and monitor the triumphs from the alternative media. As a matter of fact you will be able to judge your impact by how much the old media tries to demonize or marginalize you. Remember how the little old ladies questioning healthcare at the town meetings were portrayed as dangerous to American civility? Hell, they made Nancy Pelosi cry. Expect much more of that with every steak driven in the heart of the welfare state.

America doesn't have to be Europe. We are an industrious people and if given just a little breathing room we will bust out and start making money. That's what we do and we do it really well. Our government has cheated on us and it's time for a divorce. We don't have to take this anymore. It's time to walk away. Living well is the best revenge. Take pride in your independence and make it something others covet. Become active and help others achieve their independence. The day will come when we are the majority and we will install a government that is subservient to our demands. Freedom and independence is the apex of the human condition and it transcends race, gender, religion, and social status. If freedom is worth fighting and dying for than it is surely worth giving up your benny for.

In writing this book I hope to inspire some people to take actions that make a difference. I hope that an entire movement will arise and drastically alter the current course of our nation. But at the very least I hope it will begin a debate and put substance to the notion of "shrinking the government." I don't think electing a smaller government is possible and I don't think armed revolution is practical. I do think the Live Free Movement, with a lot of hard work and dedication can succeed. I hope in the very least you will think about it and maybe take a few baby steps in your own life to Live Free.

Live Free my friends, Live Free.

www.ingramcontent.com/pod-product-compliance
Lightning Source LLC
Chambersburg PA
CBHW060240290526
45789CB00001B/125